American Sign Language at Home

American Sign Language at Home
A Family Curriculum

For families embarking on an incredible journey of language
learning and bonding with their deaf child

Razi M. Zarchy and Leah C. Geer

Solificatio
Second paperback edition June 2023

Book design by Sheena Stuart-Milburn
Illustrations by Youmee Lee

ISBN 979-8-9858781-2-7 (paperback)
ISBN 979-8-9858781-3-4 (e-book)
www.aslathome.org

Table of Contents

Foreword

Dear parents and families of deaf children:

Learning a new language can be terrifying.

However, when you learn American Sign Language (ASL) to communicate with a deaf child, you are starting a momentous journey.

My mother was a young woman from King City, a rural California town of about 7,000 people.[1] Before I was born, she had never met a deaf person. Despite her lack of exposure to the deaf community and experiences outside of her small town, as soon as my mom found out she had a deaf child, she did not waste any time opening an ASL book. And this made all the difference in my life.

It was through the shared language of ASL that my mother and I built our relationship. ASL provided a powerful language foundation that allowed me to earn a doctoral degree and succeed in my adult life.

My experience with my mom inspired me to study parents who learned ASL for their deaf children. In my research,[2] the common denominator among all the parents I interviewed was acceptance.

Accepting a child's deafness allowed parents to overcome fears and barriers associated with learning ASL and to recognize that ASL was the gateway to having a relationship with their children. These parents wanted to understand their children when they came home from school. They were determined to teach and impart their values to them. ASL was the key to ensuring all of that happened.

A child's deafness is neither something to fear nor mourn. Instead, it is a gift to be celebrated. With the right support and a strong language foundation, a deaf child's intelligence and imagination flourish in amazing and creative ways. ASL creates an unbreakable bond in the family. Deafness comes with a culture and community ready to embrace new parents and deaf children.

Deafness does not mean the end of a parent's dream of a perfect child. Their child is still perfect, with the only difference being that they can also speak with their hands.

One of the most important and interesting parts of my research was meeting with parents of deaf children who were now adults. They had already gone through the full process of raising their children, along with the tribulations and triumphs typically found in parenthood. Each parent testified to the value of learning ASL. Doing this allowed them to continue to have rich relationships with their children and even their grandchildren.

In contrast, parents with younger deaf children expressed doubt, skepticism, and anxiety. Should they really learn ASL, or should they look at other "options"? Were they doing enough? Were they learning ASL quickly enough?

The answer is that the first step is often the biggest and most difficult one to undertake. If parents of younger children spoke with parents of older children and deaf adults, they would discover that learning ASL truly does pay off and change lives.

Learning any language can be intimidating, and ASL is no exception. But by picking up this book, you have taken that big first step and accepted that you are in for a journey. An exciting, fulfilling journey. You are in the right place. There is a community of educators, professionals, and Deaf adults out there ready to support you. By learning ASL, you will change your child's life for the better, as my mother changed mine.

–Dr. Nate Dutra

What's New in this Edition

When we released the first edition of this curriculum in July 2020, we knew immediately that there would need to be a second edition. There was no way we could write as much as we envisioned before the school year began that fall. So, we released four chapters structured around four routines in the daily lives of young children (mealtime, bath time, diaper changes, and book sharing), committing to working on eight more in the following months.

True to our promise, this edition brings readers eight new chapters with eight more daily routines, language enrichment techniques, and discussions of Deaf Community Cultural Wealth, the ways in which Deaf Culture can add richness and resources to the lives of deaf children and their families. Routines 1-4 from the first edition are the same, but we rearranged some of the language enrichment techniques to better scaffold them, ensuring they build on one another in a natural sequence.

Following Yosso and Fleischer et al.,[4] there are six types of cultural wealth, only four of which were briefly introduced with discussion prompts in the first edition. In the current edition, we include introductions to the remaining two types of cultural wealth. In chapters 7-12, we take a deeper dive into them, with specific examples of how they apply to deaf children and/or their families. We also share specific resources for families.

We have added new sections distinguishing our curriculum from "baby sign," describing the importance of routine-based learning, and giving justifications for our decision to teach mostly core vocabulary.

In our first edition, we included lessons on fingerspelling in each of the first four chapters. While we believe (and as evidence supports[5,6]) that it is never too early to fingerspell with a young one, feedback suggests that this particular skill might not be a high priority for some beginning language learners with young children. To address this, we have relocated our fingerspelling content to an appendix. This way, some learners can focus on other aspects of ASL learning, but those who wish to start exploring fingerspelling have a means to do so. By the time learners get to chapter 12, we hope that everyone will feel more prepared to begin learning about fingerspelling.

Finally, we have a second appendix with expanded vocabulary from the first four chapters, developed in response to a teacher's request for vocabulary sheets. We now have these sheets available in color (with GIFs) and black and white (good for printing) in our online store. In the process of making these, we decided to include additional vocabulary, which we are making available to all readers.

Introduction

Instructional materials needed for using this curriculum

There are several digital resources listed in each chapter, as well as links to supplementary materials. For readers using an e-book, you can click live links as you go. For readers using a paperback, please scan the QR code at the beginning of each chapter, which will lead you to a webpage with the resources for that chapter. You can access the curriculum materials for all chapters here: https://www.aslathome.org/curriculum-materials (or with the QR code in **Figure 0.1a**).

The materials for the introduction are available here: Introduction (or with the QR code in **Figure 0.1b**).

The ASL at Home Student Workbook (QR code in **Figure 0.1c**) includes worksheets necessary for the receptive practice, reflections, and other activities. They can be completed electronically or printed out.

Figure 0.1: QR codes for the Introduction. (a) Curriculum Materials webpage: the site with all the materials needed for this curriculum. We recommend bookmarking this page in your favorite browser! (b) Materials specifically mentioned in the introduction. (c) Student workbook needed for this curriculum. If you prefer to interact with this digitally, we recommend downloading it once and saving it somewhere you can access it easily. Alternatively, if you prefer to print the workbook, you can print it all at once or one section at a time.

Figure 0.1a

Figure 0.1b

Figure 0.1c

Motivation behind developing this book

We designed this book for families who have children in early intervention (birth to three years) deaf education programs. Families may venture into this text on their own or with support from their early intervention team, whether through home- or center-based practice or on an individual or small-group basis. Early intervention professionals, such as teachers of the deaf, speech-language pathologists, deaf mentors/coaches, American Sign Language (ASL) specialists, and more, may use this curriculum to support families in their journeys and bring their own unique strengths to the learning process. It can also be used to teach the families of older children, though the topics may need to be adjusted to be age appropriate.

This curriculum centers around daily routines in the lives of young children. It includes videos of highly proficient deaf signers, providing high-quality language models and hands-on activities and worksheets. It also provides guidance on language techniques that families can use with their children at home, along with the rationale behind the techniques and related discussion questions to get them started right away.

Evidence shows that access to a first language, as early in life as possible, is crucial for deaf children to develop language skills commensurate with that of their hearing peers.[7] For sighted deaf children, ASL is entirely accessible through the visual medium, regardless of hearing status. In contrast, access to oral languages can vary depending on a child's unique hearing status and listening device usage. (See **Breakout Box 0.1** for more information on DeafBlind signers and Tactile ASL.) This curriculum is a unique tool to allow hearing families to communicate with their deaf child and to help them be among the first language teachers for their children. Research has shown the importance of families talking with their hearing babies. Deaf children are entitled to the same experience with their hearing families. This curriculum helps to facilitate that.

> **Breakout Box 0.1:** DeafBlind signers and Tactile ASL
>
> Sighted deaf children are those with typical vision. These children can acquire visual languages effortlessly when given adequate exposure. DeafBlind children, or deaf children with reduced vision, may benefit from language accessible through touch, or "tactile language." In this type of ASL, the "listener" puts their hands on the signer's hands in order to understand the message. While there are similarities between Visual ASL (VASL) and Tactile ASL (TASL), there are also significant differences.[8-12] In future editions, we hope to include a section on TASL and the protactile movement. Read more at this link: Protactile Research Network (QR code **Figure 0.1b**).

The need for this curriculum

Up to ninety-five percent of deaf and hard of hearing babies are born to hearing parents.[13] Many families want to offer their child multiple language-learning opportunities to optimize language access and acquisition. For those who want their child to acquire ASL but also need to learn the language themselves, the task can seem daunting. While there are many resources available for learning ASL, few specifically serve the hearing family of a young deaf child. Some existing resources include: community-based, in-person classes; in-person and online college-level classes; online self-driven programs for parents; in-person and online deaf mentoring sessions; one-time learning events; and more. We developed this book to fill some of the gaps left by those resources. (Using *ASL at Home* in conjunction with any of these other resources is absolutely fine!)

Community-based, in-person classes can only reach so many families, since registration is often limited and the classes take place at a specific day and time. Parents may not have childcare or work schedules that permit them to take classes while their children are still young. College-level classes have some of the same barriers, plus the tuition and registration process can be cost-prohibitive or administratively overwhelming. Further, most courses are designed to teach ASL in a format similar to other foreign language courses, starting with introductions and other conversational skills that are most useful for communication between adults. Such an approach is not immediately applicable to families of young children who need language for engaging in daily routines.

Some educational programs provide Deaf Mentors (also known as Deaf Coaches), deaf adults who provide home-based ASL instruction, but many programs do not have them or are unable to provide them after a child turns three years of age. Additionally, Deaf Mentors may benefit from having a structured curriculum to guide their ASL instruction and family support.

ASL at Home is a beginning-level curriculum for families who are just starting on their ASL-learning journey. Our hope is that *ASL at Home* will provide families with the infant- and child-directed language foundation and confidence to continue their learning through other classes and learning opportunities. Families will not be fluent after completing this curriculum, but they will have a solid foundation on which to continue their language-learning journey with their deaf child.

Structure of the book and how to use it

Each lesson is organized around a routine that is common in most young children's days. This edition is geared toward families of children around three years of age and under. However, some of the routines will also apply to older children who are just starting to acquire their first language.

When a family uses *ASL at Home* in collaboration with an early intervention team, lessons can be conducted during a single home visit or center-based class, or they might be stretched over several visits. Depending on the structure of the early intervention program, visits might take place daily, weekly, monthly, or at some other frequency. Of course, if only addressed monthly, ASL skills will progress very slowly. It is up to the family and the provider to determine how often to meet and how quickly to progress. Any lesson may be reviewed an unlimited number of times.

Like any language, ASL cannot be learned passively. We encourage users to actively engage with the instructional videos. Sign along with the expressive sentences and pause them to review new vocabulary. After mastering the sentences we provide, use the sample scenarios accompanying each language enrichment technique to generate new sentences. This will help you continue developing and challenging your expressive language skills.

Lesson structure

Each lesson includes the sections listed below and accompanying instructional videos. Again, to access the videos, click the links on your e-reader or scan the QR code at the beginning of each chapter to access all videos and materials.

The purpose of these sections is to provide background information on each topic and rationale for including it in the curriculum.

1. Vocabulary
2. Sentence practice
3. Receptive practice
4. Language enrichment technique
5. Deaf Community Cultural Wealth

1. Vocabulary

Each lesson includes a video demonstrating key vocabulary words per theme or daily routine. Only eight to twelve vocabulary items are provided, to avoid giving too much to memorize all at once. As families master this initial vocabulary, they may look up additional relevant words and add them to the practice opportunities later in the lesson.

2. Sentence practice

This section combines the lesson vocabulary into short phrases and sentences. The goal is to encourage families to start using new signs immediately by providing discussion topics. Sign along while working through this section!

Since some new vocabulary is introduced that was not explicitly taught in the vocabulary section, this video is captioned. To learn how to turn the captions on/off and how to specify caption preferences, click the link or scan the QR code **Figure 0.1b**: How to Turn On Captions in YouTube. You can also adjust the speed of video playback. To do so, click the cog symbol next to the CC (captioning) symbol and select your preferred playback speed.

Sentence practice encourages families to communicate with their children at a higher linguistic level than single words. Children acquire receptive language skills that are higher than what they are able to produce expressively. In addition, because sign languages take place in a different language modality than most families' home language, sentence practice provides multiple opportunities to acquire greater coordination and fluency in that new modality. This curriculum provides families with the opportunity to practice sentences from the very beginning.

3. Receptive practice

Receptive practice includes watching videos for comprehension. Learners watch the video, then either fill in blanks or translate an entire sentence in the student workbook. For readers using an e-book, click this link to the ASL at Home Student Workbook. For readers using a physical copy, scan the QR code in **Figure 0.1c**. The receptive practice section is not captioned, because the goal is to challenge learners' comprehension skills. We recommend either downloading and saving the workbook only once or printing it, whichever is most convenient. Then, readers can fill it out as they work through the curriculum.

The purpose of receptive practice is to give the family opportunities to practice ASL comprehension. Receptive practice is especially important because many families are not actively involved in the deaf community, and the deaf or hard of hearing individuals they interact with most often are their own children. To prepare families for when their children start producing language of their own, we want them to be ready to understand it.

Each lesson also provides opportunities to expand upon learners' receptive skills, by modeling vocabulary not specifically targeted in *ASL at Home*. Translations for such signs are available as part of the activities; for example, in the sentence "I like apples," if only "like" is taught, the fill-in-the-blank might read "I _____ apples." The answers to the receptive practice exercises are available at the back of this book. We encourage learners to check their answers as they go along and use them to guide their review and refine their receptive language skills.

4. Language enrichment technique lesson

The language enrichment technique lesson includes four sections: a language enrichment technique, the rationale behind the technique, sample scenarios, and homework. The techniques are based on evidence-based language therapy practices used by speech-language pathologists and other educators to promote children's language acquisition. The goal of this section is for the provider and family to discuss each technique and its rationale, then practice the technique by responding to the questions in the sample scenarios.

To serve as a reminder between sessions to engage in this and the other activities introduced in each chapter, we have made refrigerator posters. Download and print your posters from the student workbook or from our website, ASLatHome.org.

5. Deaf Community Cultural Wealth (DCCW) lesson

Dr. Tara Yosso wrote about community cultural wealth. Also known as "cultural capital," cultural wealth is an "array of knowledge, skills, abilities and contacts possessed and utilized by Communities of Color to survive and resist macro and micro-forms of oppression" (p. 77).[3] Yosso highlighted the ways in which marginalized children's talents are overlooked because they do not conform to expected norms (norms based on white hearing children, mostly from upper middle class families). Deaf Community Cultural Wealth (DCCW) extends Yosso's work and directly applies it to deaf communities.[4] DCCW asserts that deaf people have their own types of cultural wealth that helps members of the deaf community "survive, if not thrive, in the dominant culture."[14]

DCCW is vital to this curriculum because deaf children are predominantly born into hearing families and raised in a hearing-centric world. As a result, most deaf children do not automatically have access to DCCW. Because these skills are central to survival in a hearing world, we want to teach families about DCCW so they can facilitate their deaf child in acquiring them.[4]

While a full discussion of the literature on DCCW is beyond the scope of this text, we would like to provide a taste of what research on DCCW has shown, to further illustrate why it is so important to include in a family-focused ASL curriculum.

A study of deaf mentorship in scientific fields[14] found that mentors who leveraged forms of cultural capital improved the mentorship experiences for deaf students. Specifically, their mentorship included things like teaching mentees how to ask for accommodations and advocate for their own access to communication. In a study of deaf community college students, the DCCW framework showed that students used various forms of cultural capital in "accessing and persisting in higher education" (p. 438).[15] The authors of these studies concluded that by framing deaf students' experiences in terms of cultural wealth instead of taking a deficit view, schools were more likely to partner with students to help them excel.[15]

Therefore, in this book, we include a section on DCCW in each chapter to encourage readers to reflect on the concept of cultural wealth and a strengths-based approach—rather than a deficit one—to embarking on an ASL and deaf-community learning journey with a young deaf child. Because DCCW is passed down from generation to generation,[4] we want to help hearing families pass down this skill set to their children.

In chapters 1-6, we define each aspect of DCCW and ask families to identify ways that they have used each type of cultural capital in their own lives. In chapters 7-12, we provide specific resources such as deaf organizations and websites that families can use to seek out additional capital for themselves and their children.

The *ASL at Home* Student Workbook

For readers using an e-book, click the link to the ASL at Home Student Workbook. For readers using a physical copy, scan the QR code in **Figure 0.1c**. The Student Workbook contains the following supplemental materials, which are required to complete the *ASL at Home* curriculum:

1. Vocabulary and sentence practice journal
2. Receptive practice and journal
3. Language enrichment technique refrigerator posters
4. Language technique reflections
5. General chapter reflections

This is not a "baby sign" book

This is not a "baby sign" book. So-called baby sign is the practice of taking words from natural sign languages that developed spontaneously in deaf communities and (often incorrectly) teaching them to hearing children to give them an advantage as they also acquire oral language.

This practice is often propagated by hearing people who have no connection to deaf people or deaf communities and who often earn a great deal of money and social praise from doing so.[16-19] Ironically, while baby sign programs are heavily marketed toward hearing parents of hearing children to enhance their oral language acquisition, parents of deaf children are often told not to sign with their children, for fear that signing will delay or prevent their children from acquiring oral language skills.[20] For these reasons, baby sign books and programs are generally seen as appropriative and exploitative.

To be clear, there is nothing wrong with hearing children learning actual ASL. What is problematic is when ASL words are changed, taken out of context by removing them from their roots in the deaf community, or circumvented completely with new "signs," which are often created for the profit of individuals who seek to make money from a language and culture that is not their own. When hearing vendors profit from hearing children learning baby signs, while many deaf children do not have the opportunity to learn a fully accessible visual language, the result is harmful to the deaf community.

This text *is* a curriculum that teaches child-directed ASL. Child-directed signing, just like child-directed speech (also known as "parentese" or "motherese"[21]) is a linguistic register,[22] or a specific way of talking to infants and children, which has been shown to facilitate language acquisition.[23-26] Our goal is to teach families skills to help provide a language-rich environment for their child to acquire ASL to the very best of their ability.

Why routine-based, family-centered teaching?

Young children learn best in their natural home environment when the adults follow their lead and teach through everyday activities.[27] When children participate in daily routines, they learn skills that they are able to generalize to other aspects of their lives. When families select goals for their child and receive routine-based early intervention support to attain those goals, they make more progress on those goals than families who receive traditional home visits.[28] The aim of *ASL at Home* is to provide families with basic ASL skills and language techniques to promote their child's language skills during daily routines. This allows both the children and the families to make faster progress in language learning. Families may learn these skills independently or through collaborative consultation with early intervention providers who participate in a routine-based approach.[29]

Why core vocabulary?

If you look through the vocabulary in *ASL at Home*, you might notice that there are very few nouns (words for a person, place, or thing). This is intentional. The vocabulary covered in this curriculum mostly includes core vocabulary, as opposed to fringe vocabulary. "Core vocabulary" refers to a relatively small collection of words that are used most commonly by people in a particular age group.[30] "Fringe vocabulary" refers to words that are used in specific activities or environments, such as words for varieties of foods or animals.[31] In a study of hearing children, just one hundred words made up 71% of the vocabulary these English-speaking children used on a daily basis at school.[32] Even for school-aged children, a great deal of life's communication requires only a small number of particularly useful words.

For toddlers, nouns are noticeably absent from core vocabularies. A study found that toddlers' most commonly used words were pronouns (words that take the place of a person, place, or thing, such as "I" or "she"), verbs (words that describe an action or state, such as "walk" or "see"), prepositions (words that describe a location or position, such as "in" or "on"), and demonstratives (words that point something out, such as "this" or "that").[31]

Nouns are some of the easiest words to locate in dictionaries, since it is often clear exactly which word is needed. For example, if a parent is reading a book to their child about a giraffe but does not yet know the ASL word for "giraffe," a dictionary search for the word "giraffe" would be helpful. However, it might not be as obvious that the word "ready" would be helpful when asking if the child is ready to turn the page.

To look up the meaning of ASL words in English, we recommend the _American Sign Language Handshape Dictionary_.[33] To look up how to sign an English word in ASL, we recommend the _Gallaudet Children's ASL Dictionary_,[34] which is available in print here or online here. To access these links when using the paperback version of this text, scan the QR code in **Figure 0.1b**.

Terminology

There are many views on how the term "deaf" should be represented in text. There is a traditional dichotomy in which "Deaf" refers to a cultural group while "deaf" refers to the medical condition; however, the reality is more nuanced.[35] Organizations such as California Educators of the Deaf (Cal-ED) have shifted to using "deaf" in an all-inclusive manner to reflect people who may identify as D/deaf, hard of hearing, deaf-disabled, DeafBlind, deaf+, or late-deafened, among many other potential identities. This is the practice we have opted to use in this curriculum.

Languages produced by the mouth and most often perceived by the ears are often referred to as "spoken" ones. However, since a number of deaf scholars advocate for using the phrase "speak sign language," to avoid confusion we refer to "oral" language throughout this book. This distinction leads nicely to another commonly misunderstood and misused term. "Verbal" refers to anything related to or consisting of words. Any language—English, Farsi, ASL—is verbal. However, the word "verbal" is often used to refer exclusively to oral languages. For example, if a child's dominant language is ASL, someone might incorrectly classify them as "non-verbal;" but if they use words, they are verbal.

Finally, some people might be accustomed to using "word" to refer to a word from an oral language and "sign" to refer to a word from a sign language. We find this distinction inappropriate. Because ASL is a natural language—just as English, Swahili, and French are natural languages—in this book we use the term "word" to refer to a unit of ASL with a distinct meaning, just as we would for a unit in any other language. In English, "cat" is the word used to refer to the animal in **Figure 0.2a**; "gato" is the Spanish word. **Figure 0.2b** is a still image of the ASL word that refers to the same animal. When we use "word" in the curriculum text, we are referring to a word in *any* language or modality.

Figure 0.2: (a) An image of a cat. (b) A still representation of the ASL word "cat."[36] (<u>Video of the sign meaning "cat" in ASL at this link</u>.)

Figure 0.2a

Figure 0.2b

Citations

To make this text as readable as possible and to ensure that we have properly attributed the work of other scholars that have informed this curriculum, we have used a numbered citation system. When you see a superscript number above a word or at the end of a sentence, it means that those claims are based on another scholar's work. A full bibliography of these original sources is included at the end of the book, including website URLs, where available.

Chapter 1: Meal Time

Instructional materials

All instructional videos and other materials for this chapter are available at this link: Chapter 1: Meal Time Materials or by scanning the QR code in **Figure 1.1**.

Figure 1.1: QR code for all chapter 1 materials.

Vocabulary

1. Eat/food (These are the same sign in ASL.)
2. Help me
3. Hungry
4. Drink
5. Thirsty
6. Want
7. Don't want
8. More
9. All done/finished
10. Like
11. Don't like

See Appendix B for expanded vocabulary (available for chapters 1-4).

> **Breakout Box 1.1:** Agreement verbs
>
> Agreement verbs are a grammatical feature of sign languages that use movement to indicate who is doing what to whom. The sign "help me" is the first agreement verb you will learn in this curriculum. You will learn several more as you progress through the book (e.g., "throw" in chapter 6 sentence practice). In the vocabulary video for this chapter, notice the direction of movement in this sign: the sign moves toward the signer, meaning "help me." If you changed the sign to move away from your body, it would mean you were helping someone else, or "help you."

Sentence practice with new vocabulary

This lesson is focused on mealtime vocabulary. Here are some short sentences showing this new vocabulary in action. Turn on the captions, and sign along with the video. Remember, all videos are available at the link/QR code provided at the beginning of the chapter. Look for new words not explicitly taught in the vocabulary above.

1. Are you hungry?
2. He likes ice cream. She doesn't like mushrooms.
3. I want more.
4. You don't want veggies.
5. Help me.
6. Do you want more? I don't want more. I'm all done.
7. I'm thirsty. I want to drink water.

Receptive practice

All receptive practice activities require the ASL at Home Student Workbook. We recommend downloading this document only once, saving your own copy, then filling it out as you work through the curriculum. Another option is to print it and complete the exercises by hand. You may access this document with the link above or by scanning the QR code from **Figure 1.1**, repeated here as **Figure 1.2**.

Figure 1.2: ASL at Home Student Workbook

Watch the receptive practice video, then write in the missing word(s) or translate the entire sentence. There may be more than one word per blank. Remember, these sentences aren't captioned. Test your comprehension! You may also check your answers at the back of the book.

1. I _____ to eat.

2. I _____ milk.

3. You _____ water.

4. _____ doesn't want a _____ .

5. _____ peas.

6. They _____.

7. _____.

Apply what you've learned: Language enrichment technique

Technique: Say What They're Thinking

Parallel Talk: Use your best guess to describe what the child is doing, seeing, thinking, or feeling.

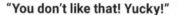

"You don't like that! Yucky!"

Why do this?

Language is much more than labeling things in the environment—children need to see full sentences in order to develop their own language skills.[37,38] By using parallel talk to expose your child to many phrases and short sentences throughout their day, you let them see what they might say if they could.[39] This is especially useful for children who are not yet producing language or multi-word utterances, because you are demonstrating their next level of language development.

Scenarios: What would you say?

Use the vocabulary we learned in this lesson to come up with a short sentence to parallel talk in the scenarios below. What is the child thinking or feeling?

1. Your child is reaching for their cup.
2. You think your child may want a certain food.
3. Your child takes a bite of food, then makes a "yucky" face.
4. Your child just finished eating what's on their plate/tray.
5. Your child is pointing at the pot from which you served their food.
6. Your child takes a bite of food then smiles at you.
7. Your child tries to put food in their mouth but keeps dropping it.
8. You start to serve your child a particular food, and they push it away.

Deaf Community Cultural Wealth

Familial Capital: My People

This type of cultural wealth has to do with people committed to a child's well-being. These are often biological, adoptive, or other extended family members, but, especially for deaf and hard of hearing children, "family" might be extended even further to include deaf teachers, mentors, and older deaf peers.

As a parent or family member of a deaf child, you can pass down your family's culture, heritage, values, and language. (See the lessons on linguistic capital in chapters 2 and 8 for more discussion on passing down languages.) To pass down your family's culture, the most important factor is the ability to communicate with your child. Language is essential for explaining the myriad complex elements of cultural values, including everything from "we don't hit our sister because it hurts her" to "for this holiday, we eat these foods and dress this way because of our people's history." Now that you are learning ASL for your child, you have taken an enormous step in preparing to share the beauty of your culture with them.

Cultivating familial capital for a deaf or hard of hearing child includes creating an environment where language is accessible and encouraged, and where deaf children can see other children and adults who are deaf. Deaf people seek out people with whom they can communicate easily and accessibly, which, in addition to biological relatives, might include deaf teachers, peers, and deaf mentors, particularly if this type of capital is not a part of the home culture. These deaf individuals can pass down deaf culture and teach children how to cultivate a positive deaf identity from a young age. In chapters 3 and 9, you will learn more about social capital ("My Network"), which you can leverage to find resources within the deaf community.

Homework/Discussion: What does your familial capital look like—who are your people? Is it only your biological/adoptive family, or do you have a "chosen family" that is also a strong part of your support system? Are there any gaps in your familial capital you wish were filled? What aspects of your family's culture are especially important for you to pass down to your child?

Breakout Box 1.2: I'm nervous about signing in front of others! What if people stare?

It's true that many hearing people are not used to seeing people sign in public (see Kolb[40] for some insights). Further, many people are curious about sign languages, which can sometimes lead them to ask you questions, which may or may not be welcome in the moment. You have the right to tell others as much or as little about your child and family as you are comfortable sharing. If you find yourself feeling stressed in such situations, it might be helpful to come up with some "scripts" for what to say when faced with them.

Brainstorm a variety of situations in which you find yourself unsure of what to say. For example:

1. A stranger comments on your child's hearing aids or cochlear implant receivers.

2. A stranger stares at you as you sign to your child at the grocery store.

3. A family member makes a negative comment about your using ASL with your child.

4. A coworker starts to ask questions that feel too intrusive about your child's hearing.

Next, come up with a few things that you could say in response. Practice the responses, so that you are ready if these situations arise. Rehearsing what you might say can help to keep your stress level down.

You may experience all or none of these situations. You may experience different scenarios altogether—every family is different! Brainstorm your own situations and develop scripts so you're prepared to handle potentially awkward questions in a way that's comfortable for you and your family.

Chapter 2: Bath Time

Recap from last time: How did it go?

Last time we learned about parallel talk. How did it go? Reflect on your experiences in the ASL at Home Student Workbook (see **Figure 1.2**, repeated here as **Figure 2.1**).

Figure 2.1: QR code for ASL at Home Student Workbook.

Instructional materials

All instructional videos and other materials for this chapter are available at this link: Chapter 2: Bath Time Materials or by scanning the QR code in **Figure 2.1**.

Figure 2.2: QR code for all chapter 2 materials.

Vocabulary

1. Bath
2. Water
    a. Pour (water) on head – WATER CL_C(pour liquid on head) (See **Breakout Box 2.1** for an explanation of classifiers and what this notation means.)
    b. Splash (water) on face – WATER CL_O>5(liquid splash on face)
    c. Splash (water) over side of tub – WATER CL_CC(tub edge) CL_55(flow over edge)
    d. (Water) dripping – WATER CL_babyO>1(drip)
    e. (Water) running from faucet – WATER CL_4(flow from faucet)
3. Dirty
4. Clean

5. Wash
    a. Wash arm
    b. Wash body
    c. Wash face
    d. Wash hair
6. Soap
7. Towel
8. Wet
9. Dry

See Appendix B for expanded vocabulary (available for chapters 1-4).

Breakout Box 2.1: Classifiers

Classifiers are unlike other types of ASL words, and there are no direct correlates in English or many other oral languages. Most words have what's known as consistent form (how a word is produced) and meaning pairing. For example, every time you pronounce the English word "dog," it refers to the same type of animal. Even if you hear the word "dog" without any context, you still know what it means. This is also true of most ASL words, including many taught in this curriculum, such as "diaper," "bath," "pants," "eat," "more," "all done," etc.

Classifiers are categories of signs for which there is no exact form-and-meaning pairing, which can be confusing. This means that the same form can represent various objects within a category, and the same object can potentially be described by different classifier forms. Classifiers can describe what something looks like, where it's located, how it moves, or how a person uses a particular object. Because of this, it is difficult to represent classifiers in text. One common way to represent ASL in writing is to use "glosses." Glosses are labels from one language used to represent the words of another language. In this case, we are using English labels to represent ASL words. While a full lesson in glossing is beyond the scope of this text, we have represented classifiers with both English translations (e.g., "Pour (water) on head") and glosses (e.g., "WATER CL_C(pour liquid on head)"). Glosses follow this format: CL_x(y). "CL" means "this is a classifier"; "x" refers to the handshape(s) used to produce a classifier; and "y" refers to the meaning of the classifier in context.

Here are some examples from a story in which one of the authors describes a memorable event from kindergarten. The handshape pictured in **Figure 2.3** can be used to describe the movement and/or location of various vehicles. In the story, this sign is produced after the sign "drive" (**Figure 2.4**). It shows the vehicle coming to a stop or parking (**Figure 2.5**). But without the word "drive" preceding it, we wouldn't know if the action of parking involved a car, a bike, or some other vehicle.

Later in the story, another type of classifier shows how a door handle is manipulated. The classifier depicts how the handle is held and pulled (**Figure 2.6**).

A final example from this story details an injury that resulted in significant bleeding. Here the classifier shows the behavior of the liquid blood (**Figure 2.7**), much like some of the classifiers for water discussed in this lesson.

Figure 2.3: Classifier handshape (CL_3) used to represent vehicles (e.g., cars, bikes, motorcycles, ATVs, etc.)

Figure 2.4: "drive to" – CL_SS(drive)

Figure 2.5: "drive to a stop" or "park" – CL_3(park)

Figure 2.6: "pull door handle" – CL_SC(grasp and pull door handle)

Figure 2.7: "blood spurting" – CL_44(blood spurting)

Even someone fluent in ASL might not recognize the full meaning of these classifier signs without context, whereas the ASL word "diaper" always refers to the same thing.

If you'd like to learn more about classifiers, and specifically how they are acquired by children, we recommend Kantor[41] and Zwitserlood.[42]

Sentence practice with new vocabulary

This lesson is focused on bath-time vocabulary. Here are some short sentences showing this new vocabulary in action. Turn on the captions, and sign along with the video. Look for new words not explicitly taught in the vocabulary above.

1. You're dirty. You need a bath.

2. You took a bath; now you're clean.

3. It's time for your bath. I'll fill up the tub.

4. Your hair is wet!

5. Time to dry off; get your towel.

6. Shoot, we're out of soap! We need to buy more!

7. Your towel smells. It's dirty.

8. Your hands are dirty. You need more soap.

9. The water is dripping. Turn it off.

10. You washed your feet. Now wash your arms.

Breakout Box 2.2: Pronouns

Pronouns are a way to refer to a noun (a person, place, or thing) without repeating its full name. This is especially helpful when the noun is already known or when you don't want to be overly repetitive. Typically, pronouns are also expected when referring to oneself ("I") or to the person one is talking to ("you"), rather than using names.

In chapter 1, you learned some personal pronouns that stand in for individuals. For example, in English, you might say, "Jon is always hungry. He likes to eat hamburgers." In this sentence, the noun introduced is "Jon" and the pronoun used to refer to Jon in the second sentence is "he." Here are some other examples of sentences with English pronouns. The personal pronoun is in **bold**.

1. **I** like strawberries. (first person singular)

2. **We** live in Sacramento. (first person plural)

3. **They** are my friends. (third person plural)

4. **She** is Julia's daughter. (third person singular, female)

5. **He** is six years old. (third person singular, male)

Notice that English has different pronouns depending on whether the pronoun stands in for the first (I, we), second (you), or third person (she, he, they). For the first and third person in English, pronouns can be singular or plural; "they" can be either singular or plural. Third person pronouns can be gendered male or female.

In ASL the pronoun categories are slightly different. Instead of first, second, and third person pronouns, there are first person pronouns and non-first-person pronouns. Like English, ASL pronouns can be singular or plural. Unlike English, ASL does not distinguish gender (i.e., there are not different signs to mean "he" or "she").

In ASL all personal pronouns are produced with an extended index finger handshape, sometimes called the 1-handshape (because this is also the handshape for the number one). See **Figure 2.8**.

Figure 2.8: 1-handshape used in the production of personal pronouns in ASL.

For personal pronouns referring to the first person, the index finger points to the signer. For personal pronouns referring to the non-first person, the index finger points away from the signer.

In this chapter, we introduce a new category of pronouns called "possessive pronouns." These are pronouns which, as the name suggests, indicate that something belongs to someone. Here are some examples in English. The possessive pronoun is in **bold**.

1. That is **my** book. (first person singular)

2. **Our** last name is Zarchy. (first person plural)

3. What is **your** name? (second person singular)

4. The book is **hers**. (third person singular, female)

5. **His** homework was late. (third person singular, male)

6. **Their** house is for sale. (third person plural)

Again, English distinguishes first (my, our), second (your), and third (her, his, their) person pronouns, gender in third person singular (her, his), and singular and plural pronouns. ASL again distinguishes first and non-first-person pronouns, as well as plural and singular ones, but it does not distinguish gender (i.e., there is no difference between pronouns meaning "his" and "hers").

Possessive pronouns in ASL are all produced with a palm-open handshape, sometimes called a closed-5 handshape (see **Figure 2.9**). First person possessive pronouns involve the palm facing the signer and non-first-person possessive pronouns involve the palm facing away from the signer.

Figure 2.9: Flat palm handshape used in the production of possessive pronouns in ASL.

Receptive practice

Watch the video, then write the missing word(s) or translate the sentence in your workbook. There might be more than one word per blank. Remember, these sentences aren't captioned. Test your comprehension!

1. __ wash my _____.
2. I'm _____. I need a _____.
3. __ were taking a _____ and accidentally spilled _____ over the edge.
4. The water is _____. Do you want it _____?
5. _____ splashed yourself in the face. Now your face is _____.
6. _____.
7. _____.
8. _____.

Apply what you've learned: Language enrichment technique

Technique: Do What They Do

Imitation: If your child uses a gesture, facial expression, sound, or sign, copy what they do.[43] After you copy them, you can add your own words or phrases. For example, if a character in the picture is frowning and your child frowns, frown back to your child before adding any words. If your child is playing with a toy, get a similar toy for yourself and imitate their actions. If they point to an image in a book, point to the same image, then look at them as if you expect them to say something about it.

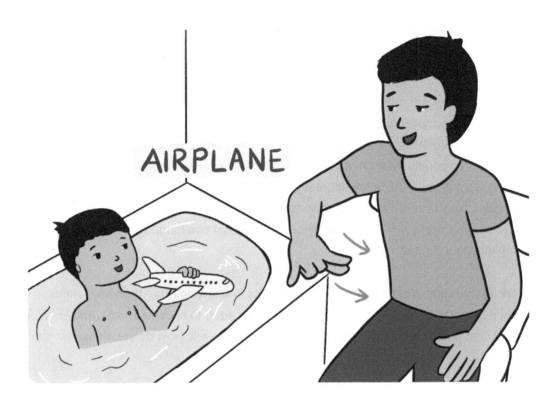

AIRPLANE

Why do this?

The key here is to copy your child. Reinforce their engagement by mirroring their actions. When you imitate your child, you teach them to imitate you, which is helpful for future language development. One thing we want to avoid is putting your child in the "hot seat" by only asking them questions, especially ones to which you have the answer. Imitating your child ensures that your communication is focused on sharing experiences together.

Scenarios: What would you do? What could you say?

Using specific actions, for each of the following scenarios describe what you could do to imitate your child to engage their interest. Based on the action you are imitating, use the vocabulary in this lesson to come up with a short sentence to engage your child with language, using parallel talk from chapter 1.

1. Your child accidentally splashes water over the edge of the tub during bath time.
2. Your child picks up a toy and water drips down from it.
3. Your child points to a toy and then to the tub of water.
4. Your child points to a dirt smudge on their body just before getting into the tub.
5. You reach for the cup you use to rinse soap from your child's hair and they smile.

Deaf Community Cultural Wealth

Linguistic Capital: Multiple Languages, Multiple Ways to Communicate

This type of cultural wealth refers to intellectual and social skills that people can attain through the use of more than one language and, in the case of children acquiring a spoken and signed language, more than one language modality. Rachel Kolb[40] wrote on this topic with respect to deaf and hard of hearing people. Many hearing people who have never encountered a deaf individual will shy away from a communication situation that doesn't involve speaking and listening; using speech is most likely the only way they know to communicate. Deaf and hard of hearing children will learn to communicate with hearing individuals in at least two languages. This gives them significant linguistic capital!

Homework/Discussion: What are some of the benefits to knowing more than one language? How might it be particularly beneficial for a deaf child or adult to know both ASL and English? It's possible for deaf people to acquire additional languages, as well. How do you think that works?

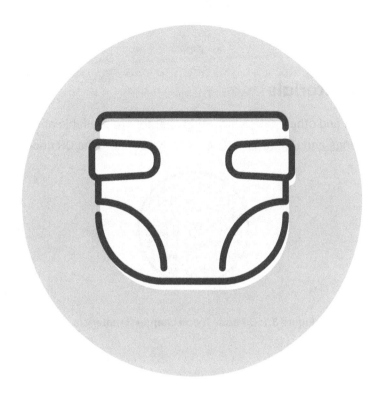

Chapter 3: Diaper Change and Bathroom Routines

Recap from last time: How did it go?

Last time we learned about imitating your child. How did it go? In your workbook, reflect on your experiences.

Instructional materials

All instructional videos and other materials for this chapter are available at this link: Chapter 3: Diaper Change and Bathroom Routines or by scanning the QR code in **Figure 3.1**.

Figure 3.1: QR code for all chapter 3 materials.

Vocabulary

1. Diaper
2. Change/exchange
3. Smelly
4. Pants
5. Wipe (action)
6. Poop
7. Throw away
8. Wash hands

See Appendix B for expanded vocabulary (available for chapters 1-4).

Sentence practice with new vocabulary

Here are some short sentences focusing on diaper-changing and bathroom-routine vocabulary in action. Turn on the captions, and sign along with the video. Look for new words not explicitly taught in the vocabulary above.

1. Are you wet? (*Raise your eyebrows, tilt your head forward, and hold the last sign to indicate that you're asking a question.*)

2. You need a diaper change.

3. You pooped. Smelly!

4. Your pants are dirty.

5. We changed your diaper; now I need to wash my hands. (*Refer to the breakout box on pronouns in chapter 2.*)

6. I throw away your dirty diaper.

7. I wiped you. Now you're clean.

Breakout Box 3.1: What if I sign it wrong?

That's fine! Learning a new language is hard, and everyone makes mistakes, particularly at first. You are already providing your child with an accessible language at home, and that's the first huge step. If you sign a word wrong, your child will learn the correct way as they get older, when they are immersed in ASL from fluent signers. What's important is that you lay down the foundation now, while they are young. Be gentle with yourself. If you make room for mistakes, you're more likely to keep your hands up and signing for more hours of the day. That's the best way for your child to learn language!

Receptive practice

Watch the videos, then write the missing word(s) or translate the entire sentence in your workbook. There may be more than one word per blank. Remember, these sentences aren't captioned. Test your comprehension!

1. You're _____. Do you need a _____ change?

2. Before you were _____. Now you're _____.

3. _____ the _____ diaper.

4. You _____. Let's go _____ your diaper.

5. _____.

Apply what you've learned: Language enrichment technique

Technique: Say It Over and Over Again

Repetition: Whatever you say, say it a lot! If you use a word or phrase every time you do a certain routine or perform a certain action, your child will start to associate the words you use with the actions and objects they represent.[44,45] If you find your child responding to a particular word or phrase more than others, keep using that word; they may be starting to understand what it means. Your continued use will reinforce its meaning. You can also pick a word or phrase and use it over and over again during every diaper change on a particular day. This can also help reinforce the meaning—through repeated exposure—of the words and phrases you're modeling for your child.

"Your diaper is stinky! Come on, let's change your diaper. Where's a clean diaper? Get a diaper, then I'll change your diaper."

DIAPER

Why do this?

Repetition helps children figure out what words (in any language) are associated with particular objects, actions, feelings, etc. Their young brains seek patterns.[46] Seeing the same word as you engage in the same routine helps them make important language connections. As an example, we saw many sentences both in the phrase and receptive practice sections that use the ASL word "diaper." If you use the word "diaper" five times during every single diaper change (which takes place numerous times a day), your child has many opportunities to associate that word with the routine of diaper changes. Ultimately, this will lead to a consistent understanding of the word "diaper" to refer to the object diaper.

Scenarios: What would you say?

Use the scenarios below to come up with short sentences to engage your child with repetitive language. You can choose a phrase to repeat over and over, or you can choose a word to use in as many different sentences as possible—the important part is the repetition.

1. Your child is fussy and pointing to their diaper.

2. You open the diaper expecting it only to be wet, but there's poop also.

3. You notice your child's pants have soaked through.

4. Your child has an explosive poop situation (you may want to think back to the "bath time" lesson for ways to respond in this situation).

5. You are finished changing your child's dirty diaper, and they reach for it.

Breakout Box 3.2: I want my child to speak! Won't signing impede their speech?

Nope! This is a common myth about sign languages. However, the research literature—and lived experience of many, many deaf individuals—shows that knowing a sign language only adds to a child's brain development, just like knowing any additional oral language.[47,48] In fact, deaf children who learn a sign language from birth are more likely to develop English skills (whether spoken or written) close to those of their hearing peers, compared to deaf children who do not have the same early access to communication. Parents of deaf children naturally tend to use more gestures with their children, which has been tied to more vocalizations in the future.[49] So go ahead and let the visual communication happen!

Deaf Community Cultural Wealth

Social Capital: My Network

This type of cultural wealth relates to having networks of people and community resources. This might include your own school district or county program, the professional affiliations of your child's educational team, including their teacher and other service providers, or other organizations. You can also look at the resources provided by your state's residential school for the deaf. Some have services that are available to all families of deaf and hard of hearing children statewide, not just those enrolled at their school.

When you are ready, your school and county providers can help you locate the many resources available. Some potential resources include: parent mentor programs to connect with other families of deaf and hard of hearing children; deaf community connections for families (ASL story times, playdates, community ASL classes); and social media connections. They can also help you find information about educational opportunities for when children get older, tackle problem-solving with listening devices, and much more. Social capital is what helps you identify the resources that will benefit you and your family most when you need them most.

Homework/Discussion: What resources do you wish you had? What do you wish you knew about raising a deaf child? Where could you find that information?

Chapter 4: Book Sharing

Recap from last time: How did it go?

Last time we learned about repeating words and sentences you use with your child. How did it go? In your workbook, reflect on your experiences.

A note on this chapter

Engaging with books is fundamental to developing eventual literacy skills. The more you read with your child now, the more you'll be able to build on that foundation as your child gets older.[50] Because the vocabulary you need for individual books varies greatly, the concepts and actions we have selected in our curriculum can apply to a wide variety of books, to get you started.

Instructional materials

All instructional videos and other materials for this chapter are available at this link: Chapter 4: Book Sharing Materials or by scanning the QR code in **Figure 4.1**.

Figure 4.1: QR code for all chapter 4 materials.

Vocabulary

1. Book
2. Read
3. Ready (two versions)
4. Turn page – BOOK CL_A(turn page)
5. Gently
6. (Interactive books)
   a. Pull tab up – BOOK CL_baby0(pull tab up)
   b. Open/close flap – BOOK CL_closed5>bent5(open flap)
   c. Pull tab sideways – BOOK CL_baby0(pull tab sideways)
7. Picture
8. What

9. What are you doing? What is it doing?
10. What happened?
11. Look at (generic)
12. Look at me
13. Look at (other object/person to the signer's left)
14. Look at the book

See Appendix B for expanded vocabulary (available for chapters 1-4).

Sentence practice with new vocabulary

Here are some short sentences focusing on book-sharing vocabulary in action. Turn on the captions, and sign along with the video. Look for new words not explicitly taught in the vocabulary above.

1. Are you ready to read a book?
2. Turn the page gently.
3. Pull that tab. See what's inside.
4. You're touching the picture.
5. What's the cow doing?
6. Look at the book.
7. Open the flap! What's inside?

Receptive practice

Watch the video, then write the missing word(s) or translate the entire sentence in your workbook. There may be more than one word per blank. Remember, these sentences aren't captioned. Test your comprehension!

1. Do you want to _____ a _____?
2. Oh no! _____?
3. ___ cat. What's he _____?
4. _____ at the _____.
5. _____.

Apply what you've learned: Language enrichment technique

Technique: Watch and Respond

Serve and Return: Notice every little thing that your child expresses, whether in words, gestures, sounds, or facial expressions, and respond in some way.[38,51] Take what your child expresses and interpret it into coherent words and sentences. This encourages your child to continue communicating with you in whatever way they can. The more you respond to your child, the more their language will grow.[43,52]

"You turned the page and...surprise!"

Why do this?

When you respond to your child's attempts at communication, you let them know that you are paying attention and that they should continue trying to communicate.[53] For more information about this technique, which is called "Serve and Return," we recommend this website: 5 Steps for Brain-Building: Serve and Return. Just like in a tennis match, when your child "serves" by communicating (by gesturing, moving, looking at you, making a facial expression, voicing, or using words in any language), you "return" their serve by responding in some way.

Scenarios: What could you do?

With the vocabulary we learned in this lesson, use the scenarios below to recognize when your child is trying to communicate with you. Then come up with short sentences to show them that you're paying attention.

1. Your child makes a "wow" face and points at a picture in a book.
2. Your child is trying to get a book down from the shelf. They can't reach it and look up at you.
3. Your child is trying to open a pull-tab on a book. They keep pulling it the wrong way, then look up at you.
4. Your child places a book on your lap, then starts paging through it.
5. You are reading the words on a book page. Your child tries to turn the page and looks up at you.

Deaf Community Cultural Wealth

Aspirational Capital: Hopes and Dreams

This type of cultural wealth refers to the ability to maintain hopes and dreams, especially in the face of real or perceived barriers. At some point in their lives, deaf and hard of hearing children will experience lack of access to communication, which can make some activities more challenging for them. Parents, siblings, and other caretakers need to remind children that, yes, some things will be more difficult in a hearing world, but that they're no less capable of doing what they've set their mind to (e.g., joining a hearing soccer team, joining the high school debate team, going to college, etc.).

Homework/Discussion: What sorts of hopes and dreams do you have for your child? How might being deaf impact their journey, if they were to follow that path? How might their hopes and dreams differ from your own, and what can you do to make sure they have plenty of aspirational capital to follow those dreams?

Chapter 5: Bedtime

Recap from last time: How did it go?

Last time we learned about watching and responding to your child. How did it go? In your workbook, reflect on your experiences.

Instructional materials

All instructional videos and other materials for this chapter are available at this link: Chapter 5: Bedtime Materials or by scanning the QR code in **Figure 5.1**.

Figure 5.1: QR code for all chapter 5 materials.

Vocabulary

1. Tuck in
2. Go to bed
3. Brush teeth
4. Sleep
5. Sleepy
6. Tired
7. Pajamas
8. Pillow
9. Blanket
10. Night

See Appendix B for expanded vocabulary (available for chapters 1-4).

Sentence practice with new vocabulary

Here are some short sentences focusing on bedtime vocabulary in action. Turn on the captions, and sign along with the video. Look for new words not explicitly taught in the vocabulary above.

1. You're sleepy. Want to get ready for bed?
2. Your pillow and blanket are dirty. We need to wash (them).
3. It's time to tuck in. Did you brush your teeth?
4. I like your pajamas. Are they comfortable?
5. It's nighttime. Time to get ready for bed.
6. Brush your teeth, then go to bed.

Receptive practice

Watch the videos, then write the missing word(s) or translate the entire sentence in your workbook. There may be more than one word per blank. Remember, these sentences aren't captioned. Test your comprehension!

1. I'm _____. I want to _____. Are you _____?
2. Do you _____ more _____?
3. I _____ that _____.
4. Good _____! I love you!
5. _____.
6. _____?

Apply what you've learned: Language enrichment technique

Technique: Get Close and Get Their Attention

The more time you spend paying attention to the same things as your child, the more their language will grow.[52,54] Here are some strategies to make sure that your child can see—and is paying attention to—the language you convey to them.

Get Face-to-Face

Make your eyes level with theirs. This might mean putting your child in a highchair, getting down on the floor with them, or using some other physical configuration.[22]

"Do you want more tickles?"

Let Them Know It's Time to Look

Some of the most common attention-getting strategies include signing "hey" (waving to your child or in front of their face) or tapping a child lightly on their shoulder or another part of their body.[26] At first, they will not know that these cues mean to look at you. It is OK to be persistent. As soon as their eyes move toward yours, make eye contact and smile to let them know that they responded well.

"It's time for bed!"

Why do this?

It can be hard to get a baby or young child to look at you long enough to sign a whole sentence. Fortunately, there are many strategies that deaf parents use, which hearing parents can also learn.[56] Young deaf children exposed to a natural sign language develop the ability to shift their eyes between a person who is signing to them and the objects around them. In fact, they do this even better than hearing children who have not been exposed to a sign language![55] However, in order to acquire this skill, they need visual language interaction. You can provide it to them!

Scenarios: What would you do to get your child's attention? Once you have their attention, what would you say?

Use the scenarios below to choose a visual attention-getting strategy, then come up with a sentence to express once you have your child's attention. Try to use a variety of strategies.

1. Your child is lying on their side, facing away from you in a toddler or twin bed, and you're coming to bring them their usual sleep toy.
2. Your baby is lying on their back in a crib, and you're about to look at a book with them.
3. Your child is facing the bathroom mirror, brushing their teeth with another adult. You're coming to tell them something.
4. Your child is playing with toys on the floor, facing away from you. You need to tell them it's time for bed.
5. (See scenario #4). You have tried one strategy, but your child didn't look at you. What else could you do to get their attention?

Deaf Community Cultural Wealth

Navigational Capital: Finding Your Way

"Navigational capital" refers to the ability to navigate situations that are not designed for deaf people. More specifically, this type of cultural capital is about being empowered to maneuver through institutions that might be reluctant to provide the support and accommodations to which a deaf child and their family are entitled.

Homework/Discussion: What sorts of systemic barriers have you and your family encountered as you have attempted to advocate for your child in educational, medical, and other settings? What do you know now that you wish you knew when your child was first identified as deaf?

Chapter 6: Playtime

Recap from last time: How did it go?

Last time we learned about getting close and getting your child's attention. How did it go? In your workbook, reflect on your experiences.

Instructional materials

All instructional videos and other materials for this chapter are available at this link: Chapter 6: Playtime Materials or by scanning the QR code in **Figure 6.1**.

Figure 6.1: QR code for all chapter 6 materials.

Vocabulary

1. Play
2. My/your turn
3. Share
4. Build
5. Big
6. Small
7. Car
8. Train
9. Block
10. Ball
11. Stacking blocks one on top of another – BLOCK CL_CC(stack blocks on top of one another)
12. Vehicle classifiers
    a. Car driving along a curvy path – CAR CL_3(moving in a zigzag manner)
    b. Two toy cars crashing – TOY CAR CL_33>SS(two cars crash together)
    c. Train car comes up behind another – TRAIN CL_CC(train car) CL_33(train car comes up behind another)

Breakout Box 6.1: Different kinds of "big" and "small"

If you compare any two languages, you will find that some concepts have direct translations, i.e., one word for one word, while for others it's not so simple. Sometimes a phrase in one language is conveyed with just a word or two in another language. At other times, a concept expressed with a single word in one language has many translations in another, depending on context. This is the case for the English terms "big" and "small." See the generic signs for "big" and "small" in **Figure 6.2**.

Figure 6.2: Left, generic sign for "big" (see video: Sign for BIG)[36]; right, generic sign for "small" (see video: Sign for SMALL).[36]

Sometimes we need to be a bit more specific about what exactly is big or small. If you are talking about a child's height for example, you would use the signs in **Figure 6.3a**, whereas if you're talking about the size of your morning coffee or your baby's milk bottle, you would use the signs in **Figure 6.3b**.

Figure 6.3

Figure 6.3a: Signs for "big" (left) and "small" (right) referring to a person's height.

Figure 6.3b: Signs for "big" (left) and "small" (right) referring to the size of a drink.

Lastly, the concepts "big" and "small" can also be conveyed through use of non-manual markers, or facial expressions. Notice the shape of the signer's mouth in the examples above. The "big" facial expression looks like pronouncing "cha," while the "small" facial expression looks like pronouncing "oooo." These non-manual markers can be applied to other ASL words and classifiers to show size modifications, as shown in the examples in **Figure 6.4a**, **Figure 6.4b**, and **Figure 6.4c**.

Figure 6.4

Figure 6.4a: Left, a classifier referring to the size of a large sandwich or hamburger. The "cha" facial expression emphasizes the large size.

Figure 6.4b: Right, the "oooo" mouth movement coupled with the sign HOUSE means "small house."

Figure 6.4c: Again, the "cha" facial expression coupled with the sign BLOCK means "large block."

Sentence practice with new vocabulary

Here are some short sentences focusing on playtime vocabulary in action. Turn on the captions, and sign along with the video. Look for new words not explicitly taught in the vocabulary above.

1. Are you two sharing your toys?
2. You're playing with the big car (moving it in a zigzag manner).
3. I'm playing with the small train.
4. My daughter loves to play with blocks (stacking them one on top of the other).
5. It's your turn; throw the ball (to me).

Receptive practice

Watch the video, then write the missing word(s) or translate the entire sentence in your workbook. There may be more than one word per blank. Remember, these sentences aren't captioned. Test your comprehension!

1. _____ is finished. _____!
2. Throw the _____.
3. More _____ please.
4. _____ a _____.
5. _____.

Apply what you've learned: Language enrichment technique

Technique: Move Your Face

Use Big Facial Expressions: You may be familiar with the concept of "baby talk," also known as "motherese" or "parentese." While parentese differs across languages and cultures, in spoken languages it often includes the adult using a wide range of pitch in their voice, simplifying words, repeating words and phrases, and other techniques. Sign languages have parentese, as well.[22,26] Instead of changing up your tone of voice to keep your child's interest, the best way to hold your deaf child's attention is to make big, dynamic facial expressions. Open your eyes and mouth wide! Play around with it!

"Wow, your train is going so fast!"

FAST

Why do this?

Big, dynamic facial expressions teach your child to look to your face for important information. As they grow and learn more, they will learn to look at a signer's face rather than at the hands, then use the facial information to understand both the ASL grammar and the feelings the person is conveying.[25, 57] If your child learns to pay attention to your face when they're very young, you can help them learn all these aspects of language just by moving your face!

Scenarios: What face could you make?

In the scenarios below, what dynamic, engaging face would you make to get your child's attention and teach them to look at your face for information?

1. Your toddler throws you a ball, but it goes over your head.
2. You are building a stack of blocks with your child, and they knock it down.
3. Your child grabs a toy from another child, then pushes them away.
4. Your child places a cherished toy in your hand.
5. Your child is playing with a baby doll, and you show them how to cradle and put it to bed.

Deaf Community Cultural Wealth

Resistant Capital: Deaf *My* Way

This form of cultural wealth derives from marginalized communities of color fighting for equal rights and true social justice. In short, it means to fight against or resist the status quo or forced assimilation. In the case of deaf children, this might entail resisting a pediatrician (with no training or expertise in language development) who tells you that signing with your child will harm their educational outcomes.

Homework/Discussion: In what ways have you had to resist information given to you by "experts" who are unfamiliar with deaf people, deaf culture, or ASL, or who have anti-deaf or anti-ASL biases?

Chapter 7: Arts, Crafts, and Sensory Activities

Recap from last time: How did it go?

Last time we learned about using big facial expressions. How did it go? In your workbook, reflect on your experiences.

Instructional materials

All instructional videos and other materials for this chapter are available at this link: Chapter 7: Arts, Crafts, and Sensory Activities Materials or by scanning the QR code in **Figure 7.1**.

Figure 7.1: QR code for all chapter 7 materials.

Vocabulary

1. Wet/dry
2. Hard/soft
3. Sticky
4. Sparkly
5. Paint
6. Paper
7. Play-Doh
8. Feel
9. We also recommend reviewing these words from previous chapters:
   a. Like/Don't like (Ch. 1)
   b. Want/Don't want (Ch. 1)
   c. Gross (Ch. 1 expanded vocabulary, see Appendix B)

Sentence practice with new vocabulary

Here are some short sentences focusing on art, craft, and sensory-activity vocabulary in action. Turn on the captions, and sign along with the video. Look for new words not explicitly taught in the vocabulary above.

1. The Play-Doh is hard because we left it out overnight.
2. The paint is wet. When it's dry, you can touch it.
3. The paper is sparkly. My son doesn't like it.
4. Go ahead, squish the Play-Doh.
5. This is sticky. Do you want to feel it?

Breakout Box 7.1: Instrument classifiers

In the chapter 2 breakout box, you learned about classifiers. These are a special type of sign in which a single form (handshape, movement, etc.) can sometimes refer to many things. Chapter 2 focused on element classifiers; specifically, the behavior of water. Other element classifiers describe the behavior of natural phenomena, such as air or fire. In contrast, instrument classifiers show how a person uses a particular object. For example, in this chapter we introduce the sign for Play-Doh. If you feel unsure of how to sign something as you and your child play with Play-Doh, just show with your hands what you are doing to it. If you want to describe squishing, flattening, or rolling it, act out the action using an instrument classifier.

Instrument classifiers aren't only used for Play-Doh. They are used any time your hands show how to handle an object or instrument, hence the name. For example, if you want to describe building a house, you'd act out the actions of hammering and using a screwdriver.

Receptive practice

Watch the video, then write the missing word(s) or translate the entire sentence in your workbook. There may be more than one word per blank. Remember, these sentences aren't captioned. Test your comprehension!

1. Cool! That's _____!
2. That _____; I like it. What is it?
3. Wait for the _____ to _____.
4. _____?
5. _____.

Apply what you've learned: Language enrichment technique

Technique: Sign in Their Bubble

Sign Where They Can See It: Make sure your child can see what you are signing. Based on studies of how deaf mothers naturally interact with their children, there are two common ways to do this when reading a book together or interacting in other situations.[22,26]

"See the big bear?"

Sign on the Child's Body

Typically, the signing space includes the signer's body and the area directly in front of them. In order to ensure that a young child can see your signs, you can include their body as part of your signing space. Put differently, you are using the child's typical signing space as your own. For example, if they are sitting on your lap, you can reach around their body to use the space in front of them to sign.

PAINT

Sign Directly on an Object

For example, when talking about turning the page, sign directly on the book itself. When signing the word "ball," place your hands on top of the picture of a ball.

Why do this?

Deaf children can only "overhear" signs that they see. For infants, adults need to make sure that their own signs take place within the small bubble of a child's visual field.[26] As children get older, they learn how to direct their eyes toward what others are showing them. When reading with your child—and interacting in other ways as well—it is crucial to ensure that they have visual access to all your signing. Doing so ensures that the language contained in those signs is received by their brain.

Scenarios: Where would you sign it?

For these scenarios, think about how you might use one of the "sign in their bubble" techniques above. Which one would work best to make sure your child sees the signs?

1. Your child is playing with Play-Doh. They want to make shapes but don't know how to use their cookie cutters.
2. Your child is playing with food in their high-chair tray, and you want to remind them to put the food in their mouth.
3. Your child is finger painting, and you want to show them how to make a handprint.
4. Your child is scribbling with crayons, and you want to show them how to draw a straight line.
5. Your child is wiping marker off the table. While standing over them, you notice a spot they missed.

Deaf Community Cultural Wealth

Familial Capital: My People

As discussed in chapter 1, this form of cultural wealth refers to a sense of connection one feels with (typically) older individuals. These might be siblings (or peers who are like older siblings) or teachers or dorm parents who play a parental role in the child's life. As also described in chapter 1, you can pass down your family culture, language, and heritage. If you are hearing, you will also need to leverage your social capital to make connections with those who can pass down deaf cultural knowledge to your child. This fusion of familial capital from your own connections and social capital from the deaf community will nurture your child's family identity and allow them to develop a strong deaf identity at the same time.

A child is far less likely to feel a profound sense of connection with someone with whom they can't communicate on their own terms. The people a child considers "family" may be highly predicated on who they feel most comfortable and themselves around. If their family does not sign, or if only certain members do, they might seek those kinship relationships elsewhere, such as from older children at school, a favorite teacher, or a dorm or cottage parent, if they attend a residential school.

Example: Omar's primary language is ASL, and he is learning English in school. He has become close with his mother and one of his siblings, because they have learned a little ASL and are able to communicate with him. His father has only learned a few signs, so—although they get along—he and Omar are not able to discuss the details of their lives. Now that Omar goes to a school for the deaf, he seeks out his "dorm parent" when he has questions about the world or his own life, since he has easy communication with him. While he has few friends near home, he has formed close, sibling-like relationships with his classmates.

Homework/Discussion: In chapter 1, you identified your own familial capital: your people. In this chapter, think about who is likely to become your child's people as they grow older. Which family members or friends will be a part of their support system growing up? Importantly, which of these people are committed to having clear, accessible communication with your child? Who else might be in your child's life as they get older? For example, if they attend school with other deaf and hard of hearing children, they may find a great deal of support in their peer group and consider those children like siblings. Regardless of their current or eventual school setting, how can you seek out peers with whom your child can communicate easily?

Here are some resources to support you in passing down your family's culture and heritage to your children. These are just a few examples, and we highly recommend doing your own further searches to find groups more local to your area:

1. Deaf Latinx organizations
   a. Deaf Latinos y Familias Organization
   b. Council de Manos

2. Black deaf culture/organizations
   a. Sankofa Archives
   b. National Black Deaf Advocates

3. Deaf Asian organizations
   a. Asian Signers
   b. Online Communities for Deaf Asian and Pacific Islanders
   c. National Asian Deaf Congress

4. Global Deaf Muslim USA
5. National Deaf Desi Association (Facebook page)
6. Deaf Jewish organizations
   a. Our Way - Yachad
   b. Jewish Deaf Community Center
   c. Jewish Deaf Congress

7. National Catholic Office for the Deaf
8. Directory of Deaf Churches & Ministries

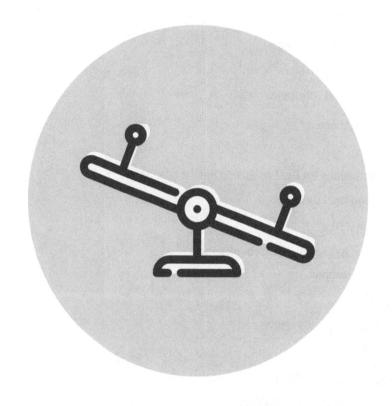

Chapter 8: Outdoors

Recap from last time: How did it go?

Last time we learned about signing in your child's bubble. How did it go? In your workbook, reflect on your experiences.

Instructional materials

All instructional videos and other materials for this chapter are available at this link: Chapter 8: Outdoors or by scanning the QR code in **Figure 8.1**.

Figure 8.1: QR code for all chapter 8 materials.

Vocabulary

1. Outside
2. Walk
3. Stroller
4. Get in stroller – CL_bentVC(get in stroller) STROLLER
5. Buckle up – CL_UU(clasp buckle at waist) CL_UU(clasp buckle between legs)
6. Run
7. Sunglasses
8. Park
9. Playground
10. See
11. Hear

Breakout Box 8.1: Lexicalized fingerspelling

To "lexicalize" means to "become a word." "Lexicalized fingerspelling" means for a fingerspelled word to become its own sign-like word. This process often results in what's called a "reduction" in some of the letters. Letters may: 1) blend together, having less clear distinction between each one; 2) be co-produced or *coarticulated*, so the sign looks like two letters at once; 3) be deleted altogether.[58,59] Fingerspelling is deeply entrenched in ASL and has been found to be more prevalent in ASL than in some other sign languages.[60] One of the vocabulary words in this chapter is "park," as in a place children play. While we have also included several other words meaning "park," we want to introduce you to the concept of lexicalized fingerspelling, since it's something you'll likely encounter as you continue your ASL-learning journey.

If you're curious about fingerspelling and ready to tackle it, we encourage you to read and practice Appendix A. If you're not ready, that appendix and associated materials will be there for you when you are.

We've created several video examples of words that are commonly fingerspelled and have become lexicalized in ASL. These are fs-PARK, fs-JOB, and fs-BACK. The "fs" designation preceding the word indicates that the word is fingerspelled. There are three versions of each word in the videos below. The first is called "careful fingerspelling," where each word is spelled out by individual letter. There is no blending, reducing, or deleting of letters. The next version is the lexicalized version. Some words are more reduced than others. The final is a slow-motion version of the lexicalized production. You might notice that even in the lexicalized version of fs-PARK (**Figure 8.2**), all the letters are still discernible. Conversely, with fs-JOB (**Figure 8.3a**) and fs-BACK (**Figure 8.4b**), only the first and final letters remain.

The rules of lexicalization—it's more than just "fast fingerspelling"—are well beyond the scope of this book, but we wanted to introduce the concept. Now if you encounter careful or lexicalized fingerspelling, you'll know what they are.

Figure 8.2: Lexicalized fingerspelling of fs-PARK. All letters remain discernible. See all videos on the webpage for Chapter 8: Outdoors or scan the QR code in **Figure 8.1** at the beginning of the chapter.

Figure 8.3

Figure 8.3a: Careful fingerspelling of the word "job." The arrow denotes the movement in the letter J (see Video Appendix A1 for the fingerspelled alphabet, also available by scanning the QR code in Appendix A), followed by individual production of the letters O and B.

Figure 8.3b: In the lexicalized version, movement in the letter J is retained, but the handshape transitions to a B-handshape.

Figure 8.4

Figure 8.4a: Careful fingerspelling of the word "back." The hand remains still as the handshapes transition from one to the other.

Figure 8.4b: In the lexicalized version, only the first and final handshapes are produced, and a forward movement is added. This sign can be produced directionally, which means in the actual direction of the movement being indicated, whether that's "back to the car," "back to the house," or "back to the bedroom."

Sentence practice with new vocabulary

Here are some short sentences focusing on outdoor vocabulary in action. Turn on the captions, and sign along with the video. Look for new words not explicitly taught in the vocabulary above.

1. Let's go for a walk outside!
2. Get in the stroller and buckle up. We're going to the playground!
3. Don't forget your sunglasses.
4. Do you see the big elephant?
5. I hear ducks quacking. Let's go find the ducks.
6. Your friend is here! Run to give them a hug!

Receptive practice

Watch these videos, then write the missing word(s) or translate the entire sentence in your workbook. There may be more than one word per blank. Remember, these sentences aren't captioned. Test your comprehension!

1. Time to take off for a _____.
2. Do you _____ the _____?
3. I _____ Daddy. Where's Daddy?
4. _____ _____ to the _____!
5. _____?

Apply what you've learned: Language enrichment technique

Technique: Give Them Choices!

Create opportunities for your child to make a choice. For example, when you know that they want to play, offer two toy options.[61] When you offer the toys, use a full sentence to name both options and ask which one your child wants. Make sure that both choices are actually available. However, they don't have to be options that you know your child wants! Offering a silly option or one you know they don't want can start a fun conversation and give your child the opportunity to practice saying "no" (instead of getting upset) in a low-pressure situation.[61,62]

"Do you want to walk or run to the swing?"

Why do this?

Children thrive when they feel a sense of control over their environment. Offering them choices gives you a chance to model language when you have their full attention, since you are offering something they want. Because it gives them some control over what happens, offering choices can also improve their behavior.[63] You can offer choices that might feel trivial to you, such as which shirt to wear or which spoon to use, but that give your child more power and agency over their life. This is an excellent way to teach them the importance of language and choice. As your child's language skills improve, you can offer longer and more complex options.

Scenarios: How could you make it a choice?

How could you use the vocabulary from this chapter to seize the moment and offer your child choices? Remember that you can offer only legitimate options, or you can offer something silly.

1. You see a playground up ahead, and your child is about to take off toward it.
2. Before your child goes to play outside, you notice that the weather has gotten chilly.
3. Your child spots a dog going for a walk with its owner.
4. You're out for a walk, and your child seems to be getting tired.
5. Your child is on a swing that they can't get down from themselves, and you're not sure if they want to keep going or not.

Deaf Community Cultural Wealth

Linguistic Capital: My Languages

Recall from chapter 2 that this type of cultural wealth refers to one's languages and/or language dialects. More is better!

Example: A common myth in deaf education is that if deaf children learn a sign language, like ASL, they will fall behind or have lower language outcomes in the majority-oral language. This is not supported by research. In fact, the opposite is true. As an example,[47] on English assessments deaf children with deaf parents who acquired ASL as a first language and then acquired English after receiving cochlear implants (CIs) performed on par with hearing children with deaf parents. This study showed that knowing ASL first is a positive for English acquisition. More language is better!

Rather than forcing families to choose one language, particularly while their child is very young, we encourage families to explore communication opportunities[64] that arise from using multiple languages in multiple modalities.

Homework/Discussion: Does your family speak Spanish? Or Farsi? Or Taiwanese? Or another language? Do you feel like you have to choose between your home language and ASL with your deaf child? You don't! They can do it all. Language builds on language. The stronger their first accessible language(s), the greater their ability to learn additional languages.[65] As long as their first language is fully accessible, they can use it as a bridge to learning others.

It is important to remember that ASL is *not* English on the hands. It is its own language, with its own vocabulary and grammar that are distinct from English. A person does not need to know English to learn ASL, and a deaf child does not need to know English to learn about your family's home language.

Here's a fun way to expose your child to English and other languages through book sharing: As you look at the pictures together, link the pictures to the written words by pointing to one, then the other. Next, sign the word in ASL. After you've done this over and over, your child will start to make the connections between them!

Check out the chapter 7 lesson on familial capital for some culture-specific resources. Deaf people from your own family's culture will be an invaluable resource for finding strategies to pass down your home language to your child. If you can learn what worked for them, you can use those same strategies in your home!

Breakout Box 8.2: Did you know that deaf people can learn multiple oral or signed languages? The stronger their first language(s), the easier it is for them to learn additional languages.[65]

Here's a story about a deaf college student and her experience learning Arabic:

- "Tory's Story: Archaeology buff, language lover, and BU's only deaf freshman"

Here are some resources for classroom accommodations to make foreign-language courses more accessible for deaf students:

- Information on foreign-language classes, from the National Deaf Center on Postsecondary Outcomes

- How to find a directory of real-time speech-to-text professionals (CART, C-Print, and TypeWell)

- Information on trilingual interpreters

Chapter 9: Cleaning Up

Recap from last time: How did it go?

Last time we learned about giving your child choices. How did it go? In your workbook, reflect on your experiences.

Instructional materials

All instructional videos and other materials for this chapter are available at this link: Chapter 9: Cleaning Up or by scanning the QR code in **Figure 9.1**.

Figure 9.1: QR code for all chapter 9 materials.

Vocabulary

1. Wait
2. Soon
3. Later
4. Not yet
5. Put away
    a. Put dishes in cabinet – CABINET CL_OO(put dishes in cabinet)
    b. Put clothes in drawer – DRAWER CL_OO(put clothes in drawer)
    c. Put toy car in open box – BOX CL_closed5closed5(open box) TOY CAR CL_C(put car in opened box)
    d. Put toys in bin – BOX CL_closed5closed5(open box) TOYS CL_O>5(put toys in bin)
6. First
7. Then
8. Put
9. Drawer
10. Box/Bin
11. Open
12. Close

Breakout Box 9.1: "First, then" and past tense

The sign FINISH (which we first introduced in chapter 1, the same sign as "all done") is used in ASL to show past tense or to show the order of events in a sequence. Unlike in English, ASL verbs don't change to show tense. There's no *walk* versus *walked* or *swim* versus *swam*. Instead, FINISH can be used before or after a verb to indicate that it already happened. If you sign BRUSH-TEETH FINISH?, it means "Did you brush your teeth (already)?"

FINISH can also be used to show a sequence of events. This is what we saw in chapter 5 with the sentence BRUSH-TEETH FINISH, GO-TO BED, which translates to, "After you've brushed your teeth, go to bed."

Another way to sequence events in ASL is with the "first, then" construction. For example, if your child is asking to do a particular activity, such as to have a snack, but you need them to pick up their toys first, you can say FIRST CLEAN-UP TOYS, THEN EAT. Alternatively, you could say EAT LATER. FIRST CLEAN-UP TOYS. A third option would be to use the FINISH structure explained above: CLEAN-UP TOYS FINISH, EAT.

We have GIFs of each of the sentences mentioned in this breakout box. For readers using a digital format, please click here to access the chapter 9 resources. For readers using a hard copy of the book, please scan the QR code in **Figure 9.1** to navigate to the chapter 9 resources.

Sentence practice with new vocabulary

Here are some short sentences focusing on clean-up vocabulary in action. Turn on the captions, and sign along with the video. Look for new words not explicitly taught in the vocabulary above.

1. It's time to clean up. Help me put your toys in the box.
2. Wait. We'll cook dinner soon.
3. It's not yet time to leave. First put your clothes in the drawer, then we'll go to the park.
4. The kitchen is dirty. We need to put the bowls and plates in the cabinet.
5. We're not (yet) done. We need to load the dishwasher.
6. We can go to Target later. First, we (we two) need to clean your room.

Receptive practice

Watch these videos, then write the missing word(s) or translate the entire sentence in your workbook. There may be more than one word per blank. Remember, these sentences aren't captioned. Test your comprehension!

1. __, you are _____ finished.
2. _____ the _____ and _____ the car in.
3. I will _____ the blocks _____.
4. Do you want me to _____ the _____?
5. _____.

Apply what you've learned: Language enrichment technique

Technique: Do It the Same!

Create Routines: You probably have home rituals that you already follow without even realizing it. For example, do you have a certain order for each step in your child's bedtime routine? Do you put on their pajamas or brush their teeth first? Start to notice your routines and identify a few that you can do the same way each time. Then choose some words or phrases to use whenever you follow those routines. Can you come up with a phrase to wrap up play and head toward bed? What could you say to your child every time they wake up from their nap? To get started, pick one daily routine along with a few fun phrases to say every day for each step of the routine. If that feels like too much at first, just pick what to say at the beginning and end of the routine, i.e., make it start and end the same way every day.[66]

"First let's clean up, then you can go play outside!"

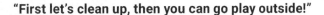

Why do this?

Routines help young children know what to expect during their day. If you use the same words and sentences each time they go through a familiar routine, they start to anticipate those words and sentences.[67] When they do, they know what they to say themselves.

Scenarios: What could you do the same?

What could you say in this part of your daily routine, every time you do it? How could you make it playful and fun, so that your child looks forward to it every day? How could you make the routine start and end the same way every time?

1. Your child wants to take out another set of toys, but there are already toys all over the floor.
2. It's time to clean up toys, and there are both cars and balls on the floor.
3. Your child just finished painting, and their face and hands are covered with paint.
4. Your child wants a snack, but there's no room on the table.
5. Your child wants to go play outside, but first they need to clean up their toys.

Deaf Community Cultural Wealth

Social Capital: My Network

Recall that this type of cultural wealth relates to having networks of people and community resources, that's why we nicknamed it "My Network." There are two examples below of what this might look like in practice.

Example 1: Rose's parents are hearing. They're learning ASL, but not as fast as Rose. Still, they know how important rich language input is, so they *called one of the members of their early intervention team*, who recommended they sign Rose up for a deaf daycare. Everyone who works there is deaf, and it is specifically designed for deaf children and their siblings, even if they're hearing.

Example 2: During the Covid-19 pandemic, Alma's parents, José and Lola, grew frustrated with the limited number of opportunities they had to socialize with other families and for Alma to interact with other deaf kids. *José and Lola reached out to their local deaf organization on social media* and found a family group that had been organized. The group had been meeting on Zoom but had recently transitioned to meeting in a local park, giving adults and kids a rich socialization opportunity.

Homework/Discussion: What resources do you wish you had? What do you wish you knew about raising a deaf child? Where could you look to find that information?

Below are some resources you might seek out in your area, both as supports for yourself and for your child. These resources are specific to the United States, but we encourage readers in other countries to seek out similar resources in their own countries.

1. Deaf community organizations

    a. The National Association of the Deaf has chapters in all US states.

    b. The American Society for Deaf Children is specifically for families, with many ASL classes and other workshops and learning opportunities.

    c. Deaf Community Services provides a list of many more organizations and resources.

2. Parent/family organizations

    a. Hands and Voices has chapters in many US states.

    b. The National Family Association for Deaf-Blind works to empower families of individuals who are deaf-blind.

3. Even if your child does not attend, state schools for the deaf often have outreach centers to support children throughout the state.

    a. The Gallaudet Regional Center nearest to you may be able to help you find local resources. We also recommend searching online for "(your state's name) school for the deaf outreach." You are likely to find some more resources there.

4. Deaf summer camps are for deaf and hard of hearing children who communicate in all languages and modalities. The camps are a great way to meet peers, and some even have family camps for younger children! Here are some resources for finding summer camps:

    a. Summer camp list from the Laurent Clerc National Deaf Education Center

    b. Summer camp list from Supporting Success for Kids with Hearing Loss

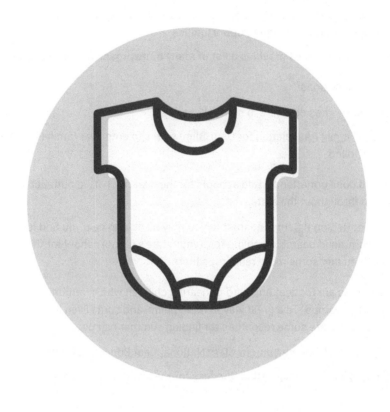

Chapter 10: Getting Dressed

Recap from last time: How did it go?

Last time we learned about creating routines and doing them the same way every time. How did it go? In your workbook, reflect on your experiences.

Instructional materials

All instructional videos and other materials for this chapter are available at this link: Chapter 10: Getting Dressed or by scanning the QR code in **Figure 10.1**.

Figure 10.1: QR code for all chapter 10 materials.

Vocabulary

1. Shirt
2. Shorts
3. Skirt
4. Dress
5. Socks
6. Shoes
7. Jacket
8. Put on and take off
   a. Take off shirt/sweatshirt – SHIRT CL_SS(take off shirt/sweatshirt)
   b. Put on/take off shoes – SHOES CL_CC(put on/take off shoes)
   c. Pull up socks – SOCKS CL_SS(pull up socks)
9. Thick/thin

10. We also recommend reviewing these words from previous chapters:

    a. Get dressed/clothes (Ch. 2 expanded vocabulary)

    b. Hot (Ch. 2 expanded vocabulary)

    c. Cold (Ch. 2 expanded vocabulary)

    d. Pants (Ch. 3)

    e. Need (Ch. 3)

    f. Ready (Ch. 4)

    g. Outside (Ch. 8)

Sentence practice with new vocabulary

Here are some short sentences focused on dressing vocabulary in action. Turn on the captions, and sign along with the video. Look for new words not explicitly taught in the vocabulary above.

1. It's cold today. You need a jacket.

2. Time to get dressed. Pick out a shirt, shorts, underwear, and socks.

3. Are you hot? Take off your sweatshirt.

4. Do you want to wear pants, shorts, or a skirt (which)?

5. That shirt is thin. You'll feel cold. Let's find one that's thicker.

6. Your shoes are wet. Let's take them off.

7. Do you prefer to wear a dress today?

Receptive practice

Watch the video, then write the missing word(s) or translate the entire sentence in your workbook. There may be more than one word per blank. Remember, these sentences aren't captioned. Test your comprehension!

1. I like your new _____.

2. Time to _____ your _____ and _____!

3. I have your _____. Come on and _____!

4. Are you ready to _____ your _____?

5. It's _____. You need _____.

6. _____. _____?

Apply what you've learned: Language enrichment technique

Technique: Take Turns!

Create Routines: Create opportunities to take turns with your child. It could be as simple as a game of peek-a-boo or as complex as a ball-play activity. Harness your child's interest by imitating them or doing whatever you can to get them to repeat an action. However possible, try to get them to do something once and repeat it. In response, repeat what you did. And there you have it! You're taking turns! Here's an example:

When your toddler pushes a car across the floor, chase the car, then push it back to them. They may not yet understand how to push it back to you. Regardless, whichever direction they push the car, chase it, and push it back to them. This establishes turn-taking and keeps your child engaged with you. You can also use parallel talk to say what they might be thinking (remember this technique from chapter 1?), making a comment about what you're doing, such as "I got it!" or "Mommy is playing!"

"Where's Mama?"   **"I see you!"**

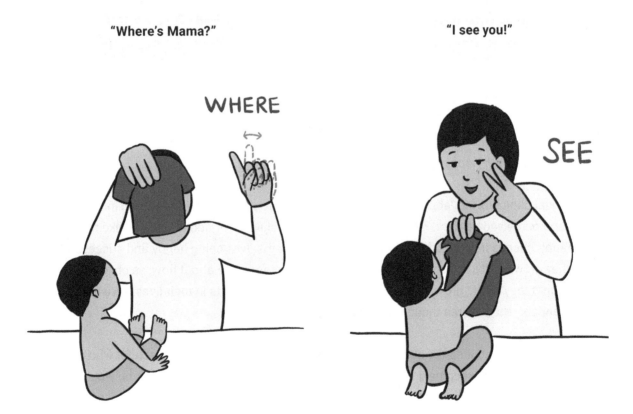

Why do this?

Turn-taking is at the heart of human interaction.[68,69] A pause in conversation with someone signals to them that it is their turn to participate. By taking turns with your child, you set up the expectation that you will respond to their attempts to engage with you and let them know you will respond to theirs.[61,67] Turn-taking games are great fun and offer many opportunities to add language to interactions, particularly because they are naturally repetitive. They create a prime opportunity to use your repetition technique from chapter 3 and say the same thing over and over again. Improving your child's turn-taking skills can even improve how often they initiate communication with both adults and other children.[70]

Scenarios: How could you start a back-and-forth?

What could you do to turn the following scenarios into turn-taking interactions? What language could you add every time you or your child takes a turn? Make it fun and silly to hold your child's interest!

1. Your child is trying to put on a beanie (hat) but can't quite get it right.
2. You're holding up a onesie to your child before putting it on them.
3. Your baby is lying on their back, looking up at you before you dress them.
4. Your child is trying to put on a shirt, but they accidentally put their arm through the head hole.
5. Your child's hood was up, but the wind blew it off their head.

Deaf Community Cultural Wealth

Aspirational Capital: Hopes and Dreams for the Future

Aspirational capital is the "ability to maintain hopes and dreams for the future, even in the face of real and perceived barriers."[3] When children see older children or adults who are like them and have happy, successful lives, they are able to imagine themselves being happy and successful when they grow up. It's not uncommon for deaf adults to reminisce about how, as children, they thought they would grow up to be hearing. Since the only adults in their lives were hearing, understandably the children thought that deaf adults did not exist!

Richard Horrell[71] described the experience of a deaf student in a mainstream school who asked if he would remain deaf when he grew up. When he was told that he would and that he would meet many deaf adults, he began sobbing. He had attributed his loneliness to his deafness, unaware that the real cause was his isolation from other deaf people.

Now that you are beginning to learn ASL, you can give your child aspirational capital by introducing them from a young age to a variety of deaf adults. This will instill on a deep level the knowledge that they can grow up to be whoever they want to be.

Aspirational capital also helps individuals realize that whatever barriers they experience as a part of their marginalized identities are intrinsic to the larger society—and not their own fault. When other deaf people share their experiences encountering communication, education, employment, and other types of barriers, you can learn how they overcame them. Perhaps even more importantly, you can see that you are not alone.

Example 1: Aspirational capital for families
Through early intervention, you invite a deaf mentor to your home. They are an early intervention provider who also teaches preschool. They have a master's degree, work full-time, and consider themselves to be a successful professional. They describe some of the barriers they experienced as a child and give suggestions for how your child can avoid them.

Example 2: Aspirational capital for children
Deaf adults in various careers visit your child's class, introducing them to different professions they might have when they grow up. Most importantly, it shows your child that there are adults like them. These adults talk about how they use their flexibility with communication to get along with both hearing and deaf coworkers.

Kenya Hameed and Jamie Howard wrote about the importance of discussing systemic racism with Black children.[72] Doing so fosters pride in themselves and helps them to understand that injustices they experience or witness do not happen because of something inherently bad about themselves. Similarly, parents of deaf children—and members of the deaf community who are involved in the children's lives—can discuss audism. Audism[2] is discrimination based on one's hearing status and is rooted in the stigma that people who can hear or act more like hearing people are inherently better than people who do not. The belief that oral languages are superior to sign languages is a type of audism.

Here are some resources for learning about audism. As your child grows, you can start to introduce the concepts they address, so that your child understands that many barriers they face are part of living in an audist society and are not their own fault.

1. Examples of audist behaviors from VAWnet
2. A TEDx talk by Dr. Peter Hauser: "Effects of Linguisticism and Audism on the Developing Deaf Person"
   a. Dr. Hauser is a deaf psychologist with a PhD. Talk about aspirational capital!
3. "Check your biases: Audism in the 21st century," recommendations by Caitlin Giammona, a speech-language pathologist who owns The Signing SLP in Northern California

Chapter 11: Family Time

Recap from last time: How did it go?

Last time we learned about creating opportunities to take turns. How did it go? In your workbook, reflect on your experiences.

Instructional materials

All instructional videos and other materials for this chapter are available at this link: Chapter 11: Family Time or by scanning the QR code in **Figure 11.1**.

Figure 11.1: QR code for all chapter 11 materials.

Vocabulary

This chapter addresses terms for talking about family. While it has more vocabulary than most chapters, the words are easily grouped. Here is a way that should make them easier to remember: In ASL, many kin terms—ones for family members—are gendered (see **Figure 11.2**). Signs for male relatives are produced at the height of the forehead. These include father, grandfather, son, and brother. Female terms are produced at the height of the chin. These include mother, grandmother, daughter, and sister. More recently, gender-neutral signs have emerged that are produced in the middle, at about the height of the ear or nose. These include parent, grandparent, and sibling. We hope these groupings are helpful for committing these new words to memory and applying them in the activities in this chapter—and, more importantly, in real life!

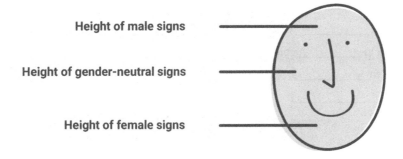

Figure 11.2: Visual representation of the location of gendered and non-gendered kin terms in ASL.

1. Family (two versions)
2. Mother/Father/Parent
3. Daughter/Son/Kid
4. Sister/Brother/Sibling
5. Grandmother/Grandfather/Grandparent
6. Love
7. Visit
8. Leave
9. Stay
10. Overnight
11. All day

Sentence practice with new vocabulary

Here are some short sentences focusing on family vocabulary in action. Turn on the captions, and sign along with the video. Look for new words not explicitly taught in the vocabulary above.

1. This weekend we're going to visit your grandparents. We'll stay all day!
2. Do you want to stay overnight with Grandpa?
3. Time to pick up your siblings from school.
4. Tell your parent you love them.
5. Do you love your brother? Give him a hug.

Receptive practice

Watch the video, then write the missing word(s) or translate the entire sentence in your workbook. There may be more than one word per blank. Remember, these sentences aren't captioned. Test your comprehension!

1. __ we will _____.
2. Our _____ will play here _____.
3. Her _____ is _____ now!
4. _____ wants you to _____, please.
5. Wait! It's not yet time to _____.
6. _____.

Apply what you've learned: Language enrichment technique

Technique: Change It Up, Then Wait!

Now that you're a master at taking turns and repetition, it's time to change it up! Engage your child in a turn-taking game that is familiar to them. Take several turns, then change one thing. You could say or do something different. The goal is to do something unexpected or especially silly to catch your child's attention. Make sure to say something when you do! Do this several more times and keep it silly! Then, wait to see how your child responds. (Remember *Watch and Respond* from chapter 4?) Their response will guide you how to respond and keep the interaction going.

Here is the example from chapter 10, with the added step of changing it up:

When your toddler pushes a car across the floor, chase it, then push it back to them. They may not yet understand how to push it back to you. Regardless, whichever direction they push it, chase it, then push it back. This establishes turn-taking to keep them engaged with you. You can also use parallel talk to say what they're thinking (remember this technique from chapter 1?) by commenting something about what you're doing, such as "I got it!" or "Mommy is playing!"

***THEN*, change it up!**

Once your child sees that you are taking turns, change something and make it silly! For example, you could:

1. Change the words/sentences that you're saying with each turn, then wait and respond to your child's response.
2. Grab a different car and push that one back instead, then wait and respond to your child's response.
3. Push the car backward, then wait and respond to your child's response.
4. Stand up and bend over to look through your legs at your child. Then push the car back, wait, and respond to their response.
5. Pretend to drive the car down the wall. Then push the car to your child, wait, and respond to their response.
6. Do anything else that changes up the activity but catches your child's attention and keeps them involved! Then wait and respond to their response.

"I love you! Yes, I love you! I love you! And I love...Daddy! And I love...brother! And I love...Grandpa! And I love...you!"

Why do this?

When you set up a turn-taking game, your child pays extra special attention to what you say in the moment you unexpectedly change it up.[67] This is a fantastic way to introduce new language in a way that they will notice and remember.

Scenarios: What could you do?

How could you change up these sample turn-taking games to do and say something silly and different?

1. Your child blows you a kiss, and you blow one back.
2. Your child points to all the people in the room and has you name them.
3. You're looking at a family photo with your child, naming the people in the picture and saying "I love _____, and I love_____," etc.
4. You're telling your child about who is coming over, listing each person.
5. Your child is running or crawling from one person to another in the living room.

Deaf Community Cultural Wealth

Navigational Capital: Finding Your Way

"Navigational capital" refers to the ability to navigate different situations that are not designed for deaf people. It can be challenging to find the resources necessary to get full access to communication and other services, but navigational capital gives individuals the knowledge to do so.

Example: A deaf student is preparing to transfer from their local community college to a four-year university in another state. When they entered community college, their vocational rehabilitation counselor helped them and their parents to register with the disabled students office to secure accommodations, including ASL interpreters, real-time captioning, note-taking assistance, and preferential seating. The counselor explained that if they later transferred to a four-year university, they would need to go through this process on their own.

Now that they are transferring, they know to look for a disabled students office—and that this office has a different name at every school. They know to ask what paperwork they will need and to ensure that the same accommodations they had at the community college will be provided.

Homework/Discussion: What sorts of systemic barriers have you (and your family) encountered as you have attempted to advocate for your child in educational, medical, and other settings? What do you know now that you wish you knew when your child was first identified as deaf?

Here are some resources for navigating the early stages of your child's identification as deaf or hard of hearing. We hope you find them helpful!

1. Audiologists who support families online:
   a. Audiology Outside the Box by Dr. Sarah Sparks
      i. Dr. Sparks provides tele-audiology services in multiple states. She also has two cochlear implants and uses ASL and English in her practice.
      ii. She provides education about person-centered care and respect for global communication (regardless of the individual's language uses and preferences) and access for all.
   b. Listen with Lindsay by Dr. Lindsay Cockburn
      i. Dr. Cockburn is very active on social media as @listenwithlindsay and frequently discusses resources available to families to navigate audiological care, language development, and more.
   c. Mama Hu Hears by Dr. Michelle Hu, who grew up using hearing aids and now has cochlear implants

      i. Dr. Hu recently published a course and workbook called *My Child Has Hearing Loss, Now What?* dedicated to supporting parents through the initial process of identification, audiological appointments, early intervention referrals, emotional processing, and more.

      ii. Dr. Hu is also very active on Instagram as @mama.hu.hears and on Facebook as @mamahuhears.

  d. <u>All About Audiology Podcast</u> by Dr. Lilach Saperstein (Every episode comes with a full transcript.)

      i. Dr. Saperstein is also a parent advocate and has a variety of other resources, retreats, and support for families. She can be found on Facebook as @lilach. saperstein.5 and on Instagram as @allaboutaudiologypodcast.

      ii. Catch the episode about *ASL at Home* <u>here</u>!

2. Most states have resources related to <u>Early Hearing Detection and Intervention (EHDI)</u>. If your state does not offer many, consider looking into and getting in touch with the resources posted for neighboring states. They might be able to refer you to something more local.

  a. These resources are especially helpful for learning how the process works in your state for identifying a child's hearing level, as well as what is expected for referral to services.

3. "Early Intervention," "Early Start," or "Part C" are terms used to describe support services provided to children under the age of three who have been identified as having a disability (including deafness or being hard of hearing) and their families.

  a. "Part C" refers to the section of the Individuals with Disabilities Education Act (IDEA)[73] that established services for families of disabled children under three years of age.

  b. These services are free, usually provided by the county, school district, regional center, or another local public agency.

  c. Here are some resources that describe early intervention services for families of deaf and hard of hearing children:

      i. <u>National Association of the Deaf (NAD)</u>

      ii. <u>National Center on Hearing Assessment and Management (NCHAM)</u>, which oversees EHDI nationwide in the United States

4. Typically, deaf and hard of hearing children who have been receiving early intervention are assessed to see what services they may qualify for after their third birthday. When they turn three, they transition from early intervention to special education.

  a. This is also often called the transition from Part C to Part B. Part B refers to the section of IDEA that established special education for children and young adults ages three to twenty-two years of age.[73]

  b. This transition can be very confusing for families. Here are some resources to learn more about what to expect. They are both based in California but may also be useful for families in other states:

      i. "<u>Turning Three Years Old</u>" from Warmline Family Resource Center

ii. "Effective Early Childhood Transitions" from the California Department of Developmental Services and the California Department of Education

Chapter 12: Pets

Recap from last time: How did it go?

Last time we learned about creating opportunities to take turns. How did it go? In your workbook, reflect on your experiences.

Instructional materials

All instructional videos and other materials for this chapter are available at this link: Chapter 12: Pets or by scanning the QR code in **Figure 12.1**.

Figure 12.1: QR code for all chapter 12 materials.

Vocabulary

1. Dog
2. Cat
3. Pet (verb)
4. Animal
5. Be careful
6. Lick
7. Feed
8. Don't/not
9. Touch
10. Classifiers for animal positions

    a. Animal in seated position – CL_bentV(animal in seated position)

    b. Animal standing on all fours – CL_44(animal standing on all fours)

    c. Animal curled up – CL_bentV(animal curled up)

Sentence practice with new vocabulary

Here are some short sentences focusing on pet-related vocabulary in action. We are also introducing some more fingerspelling. Remember to refer to Appendix A to go over fingerspelling basics. When you're ready, turn on the captions, and sign along with the video. Look for new words not explicitly taught in the vocabulary above (and practice your fingerspelling).

1. That dog is nice. His name is Max.
2. Do you want to pet the cat? Be gentle.
3. Darcy is curled up sleeping. Leave (her alone). Don't touch (her).
4. Jamie is silly, always licking (my face)! (See Appendix B with expanded vocabulary for chapter 4.)
5. Want to help me feed the dog?
6. The cat standing there is named Chloe.

Receptive practice

Watch the video, then write the missing word(s) or translate the entire sentence in your workbook. There may be more than one word per blank. Remember, these sentences aren't captioned. Test your comprehension!

1. Do you want to _____ the _____?
2. The six _____ eat dry _____.
3. The _____ is _____ sleeping.
4. _____ is a good _____! She's _____.
5. _____!

Apply what you've learned: Language enrichment technique

Technique: Stretch It Out!

Expand and Recast: If your child points, respond with a word or short phrase.[38,51] If your child says a single word, respond with a short phrase or sentence. If your child says a short phrase, respond with a full sentence. The important part is to use *their* words in your response. For example, if your child signs "dog," you can respond "The dog is eating!" This is called an "expansion." You can also add even more language, such as a follow-up question: "The dog is eating! Do you think he likes it?" That is called a "recast,"[74] because you are expanding on what your child said and adding something new.

Here's another example of an expansion: If your child sees a fish in a tank and signs "water," you could expand on what they said by signing, "The fish is swimming in the water!" Just remember: Whatever they say, mirror their word(s) back, one or two steps higher than how they said it.

"That's right, the cat is sleeping! Shhh, don't wake them."

Why do this?

Children learn language best when adults use language that is one step above theirs.[43] In particular, using their own words rephrased into more complete sentences shows children how to fill in grammar that they are still learning to use. For example, if your child is using single words, repeating their one word while adding two to three additional ones can help push them to the two-word stage. If your child is not yet using words, responding to their looks and points with one or two words helps them learn what they could say when they're ready.[75]

Scenarios: What would you say?

How could you expand on your child's signs to mirror language that is one step higher? You can just expand (make the language more complete), or you can recast (make it more complete, then add a follow-up comment or question).

1. Your child sees your dog eating and signs "DOG."
2. Your child notices that the cat is sleeping and signs "CAT SLEEP."
3. Your child sees an unfamiliar dog while out on a walk and signs "BE-CAREFUL."
4. After watching your pet fish, your child looks at you and makes a "fishy face."
5. A cat starts walking up to your child, and your child signs "CAT."

Deaf Community Cultural Wealth

Resistant Capital: Deaf *My* Way

This form of cultural wealth is about minoritized communities resisting dominant narratives about how people should be. As it applies to deaf people, this most often refers to resisting the dominant insistence on being hearing or using oral language.

A prominent example of resistant capital occurred in 1988, when a group of deaf students at Gallaudet University organized a week-long protest after the school's board of trustees named a hearing individual who did not know ASL as the next president. This protest received worldwide attention (at a time well before the advent of rapid, twenty-four-hour news cycles) and came to be known as "Deaf President Now," or "DPN." The key tenet of this protest was self-determination. Rather than let hearing people make decisions for deaf people, the deaf students rose up to resist having hearing people make decisions on their behalf.

A more personal form of resistance is for deaf people to wear listening devices only when they want to, rather when it is convenient for a hearing person's communication preferences (i.e., the use of oral language).

Homework/Discussion: In what ways have you had to resist information given to you by "experts" who are unfamiliar with deaf people, deaf culture, ASL, and/or have anti-deaf/anti-ASL biases?

Additional Resources: Here are some resources you might find interesting and helpful for furthering your understanding of resistant capital. They help illustrate how some deaf adults have resisted dominant hearing narratives and norms by living their lives as they see fit.

1. Christine Sun Kim, sound artist: "The enchanting music of sign language"
2. Heather Artinian, deaf lawyer: "Not the hearing or Deaf world | TEDxGeorgetown"
3. *What the Deaf?!*, a podcast by two deaf friends who explore a variety of topics. One video examines the question "Is There A 'Right' Way To Be Deaf?"
4. De'VIA (Deaf View/Image Art)[76] is a type of art that "expresses the Deaf experience from a cultural, linguistic, and intersectional point of view" and "challenge[s] oppression and celebrate[s Deaf] culture." De'VIA is a common way to express resistance to dominant narratives. Some prominent De'VIA artists include Maureen Klusza, Nancy Rourke, David Call, and Betty Miller.
5. Deafhood, a term coined by British deaf researcher Paddy Ladd

Future Directions

This twelve-lesson curriculum is the first in what we hope will become a several-book series. As we have noted, the goal of this curriculum is to embed rich language in your child's environment. Thanks to thoughtful, detailed feedback from our readers, we have revised the introduction and first four chapters of this curriculum, then added 200% more content to this edition. In fact, it was our readers who helped us select the routines for the new chapters!

In the short term, we look forward to sharing this new edition with providers and families. In the long term, our next goal is to develop a similar curriculum for families of older children, in which we will also begin to address the needs of signers with more intermediate-level ASL skills. Thank you for being part of this journey with us!

If you also aim to converse in ASL on a wide range of topics with other adults—as well as with your deaf child—*ASL at Home* can serve as a jumping-off point for more advanced courses. Here are some resources for continuing your ASL learning:

1. Evermore ASL Immersion Academy: ASL instruction for families, academic support for children, and more
2. American Society for Deaf Children
    a. Online ASL classes and webinars on many topics
    b. SignOn with ASDC: one-on-one tutoring with deaf ambassadors (five sessions free with ASDC membership)
3. ASL Connect (Gallaudet University): Online courses for college credit and summer residency program
4. Community college classes: Often available through your local institution(s)
5. The Signing Room: an online, immersive ASL environment for families and professionals looking to move beyond the "beginner" phase

Receptive Practice Answers

Hopefully you have gone through the videos and tested your ASL comprehension based on each of the themed lessons in the text. In this section, use the answers provided for each of the translation questions to check your work. If you got the right answer, great! If you didn't, what went wrong? Use these answers to learn from your language-learning mistakes. And remember, there is absolutely nothing wrong with being at the beginning of your ASL-learning journey! Learning a language is hard, and it took courage to get to this point. It will take even more courage to put yourself out there, make mistakes, learn from those mistakes, and keep going. Your ASL will be better because of the mistakes you make along the way.

Chapter 1

1. I want to eat.
2. I like milk.
3. You drink water.
4. She doesn't want a drink.
5. You don't like peas.
6. They want more food.
7. You help me.

Chapter 2

1. I wash my hair.
2. I'm wet. I need a towel.
3. You were taking a bath and accidentally spilled water over the edge.
4. The water is dripping. Do you want it on all the way?
5. You splashed yourself in the face. Now your face is wet.
6. I don't like baths.
7. I want more soap.
8. You are dry.

Chapter 3

1. You're smelly. Do you need a diaper change?
2. Before you were wet. Now you're clean.
3. Throw away the dirty diaper.
4. You pooped. Let's go change your diaper.
5. We're finished changing your diaper!

Chapter 4

1. Do you want to read a book?
2. You're touching the page.
3. Oh no! What happened?
4. Silly cat. What's he doing?
5. Look at the picture.
6. I want to open the flap.

Chapter 5

1. I'm tired. I want to sleep. Are you tired?
2. Do you want more pillows?
3. I don't like that blanket.
4. Good night! I love you.
5. Time to sleep!
6. Are you tired?

Chapter 6

1. My turn is finished. Your turn!
2. Throw the ball.
3. More small blocks please.
4. Build a big train.
5. The car is driving on a bumpy road.

Chapter 7

1. Cool! That's shiny!
2. That feels soft. I like it. What is it?
3. Wait for the paint to dry.
4. You don't want more paper?
5. The paint is sticky, gross.

Chapter 8

1. Time to take off for a walk.
2. Do you see the playground?
3. I hear Daddy. Where's Daddy?
4. Go run to the park!
5. Do you want to play outside?

Chapter 9

1. Wait, you are not yet finished.
2. Open the bin and put the car in.
3. I will help you put away the blocks later.
4. Do you want to close the box?
5. First clean up, then eat.

Chapter 10

1. I like your skirt.
2. Time to put on your socks and shoes!
3. I have your dress. Come on and get dressed.
4. Are you ready to take off your shirt?
5. It's hot outside. You need shorts.
6. That jacket is thick. Are you hot?

Chapter 11

1. Soon we will visit Grandma.
2. Our family will play here all day.
3. Her daughter is big now!
4. Daddy wants you to stay, please.
5. Wait! It's not yet time to leave.
6. Your sister loves you.

Chapter 12

1. Do you want to pet the dog?
2. The six cats eat dry kibble.
3. The animal is lying down sleeping.
4. Lucy is a good dog! She's sitting (facing me).
5. Be careful and don't touch Nova!

Acknowledgements

We are so grateful to everyone who contributed to bringing this curriculum to life, both in its original, completely homegrown version released in 2020 and the current version.

We would first like to thank the families in Razi's school district who have attended the family class that he founded, and that Leah taught for a semester (and hopes to teach again in the future). It was through working with these families that we realized that a curriculum of this type was so sorely needed to target this unique population. Many thanks to them for sharing their journeys with us and providing input on what the most functional curriculum would look like for them.

We want to thank our editor and publisher, Matthew Félix, and our artists, Sheena Stuart-Milburn (with support from Brian Milburn) of Design to Glow and Youmee Lee, for helping us realize our vision. We thank them for believing in our program and being so enthusiastic about bringing this version of *ASL at Home* to life. Thanks to our deaf language models, Diego Guerra, Lauren Hostovsky, Romduol Ngov, and Tess Dozier, for bringing fresh faces to our instructional videos and for sharing their time and passion for ASL.

We also want to thank everyone who contributed to our Kickstarter campaign, without whom publishing this book would not have been possible (or would have been significantly delayed). In particular, we want to recognize financial (and parental) support from Bill and Susan Zarchy and Rod and Maria Geer, as well as our Bronze Level Backers, the Evermore ASL Immersion Academy (**Figure A.1**) and Dr. Ellen Schneiderman of the California State University, Northridge (**Figure A.2**) Deaf Education Program.

Figure A.1: (Left) Logo for the Evermore ASL Immersion Academy; (right) QR code for the Evermore website.

Figure A.2: (Left) Logo for California State University, Northridge; (middle) QR code for the Deaf/Hard of Hearing Teaching Credential website; (right) QR code for the MA in Special Education with emphasis in Deaf/Hard of Hearing website.

Appendices

Appendix A: Fingerspelling

All video resources are available in <u>Appendix A</u>, or you can scan the QR code in **Figure AA.1**.

Figure AA.1: QR code for Appendix A materials.

Fingerspelling lesson 1

Fingerspelling is a system used in some sign languages to represent written languages that are in contact with a particular sign language. In the case of ASL, fingerspelling represents written English words with the hands (though it can also be used to represent any other language which uses the same writing system, such as Spanish). <u>Video Appendix A1</u> demonstrates the ASL alphabet in full. Warm up your fingers by signing along with the video!

It's never too early to expose children to fingerspelling, even if they're not yet learning to read. Research shows that children perceive fingerspelling holistically; they think of it as just another word.[77] When children are very young, typically their attempts to produce fingerspelling will retain the most salient movements of a fingerspelled word, even if each of the specific letters is not individually produced.

As children are exposed to words in print over time, they make the association between manual and written characters.[78] There is some evidence to suggest that fingerspelling facilitates reading development and acquisition of new vocabulary, but more work is needed to truly understand how fingerspelling interacts with literacy.[79,80] There is no downside to fingerspelling with little ones, regardless of their age.

Fingerspelling lesson 2

This lesson reviews letters produced with a primarily closed fist: A, E, I, O, S, T, M, and N. Watch <u>Video Appendix A2</u> and sign along!

Here's a challenge for this lesson: When you're in your car and stopped at a light or as you ride the bus or commuter train, practice spelling the letter portions of license plates and the names of restaurants and businesses you see out the window.

Fingerspelling lesson 3

This lesson focuses on letters produced with a primarily open hand with various fingers extended from the fist: B, C, D, F, K, L, R, U, V, W, and X. Watch Video Appendix A3 and sign along!

In the previous lesson, we challenged you to practice fingerspelling in your car or on the bus or commuter train. How did you do? There may have been some letters you forgot. That's OK. Keep practicing, and the process will become more automated with time.

Here's a challenge for this lesson: Review the remaining letters in this lesson and keep practicing with everything you see. If you see a table in your environment, spell "table." If you see a candle in a window, spell "candle" and then "window." It doesn't matter what you spell. The point of this exercise is to get your fingers used to forming different letter combinations that happen in actual words (as opposed to repeatedly practicing the alphabet). Not only does this type of practice increase your finger mobility, but it also helps automate the process of fingerspelling so you don't have to think about how to form each of the letters; you do it automatically. Don't worry about speed. That comes with time.

Fingerspelling lesson 4

This lesson presents the letters P, Q, Y, and Z in Video Appendix A4. Notice that the handshape for the letter P is the same as the letter K. The difference is the orientation of the wrist. In K, the wrist is slightly extended (bent backward); the hand faces upward. In P, the wrist is bent, and the hand faces downward. The letter Y can have either a neutral or flexed (bent forward) wrist. The flexed wrist posture is most common in the middle and ends of words. In the letter Z, the index finger traces the shape of the letter Z in the air. Watch the accompanying video and sign along!

Here's a challenge for this lesson: Work on clear, smooth fingerspelling. Most letters are produced with the palm out, facing the person you're talking to. To produce fingerspelling clearly, gently transition from letter to letter without bouncing.

This lesson introduces letters that require the orientation of the palm—the direction your palm faces—to change. Again, the goal is to move only the joints that are necessary. Relax your shoulder; make sure it is not moving as you fingerspell. Your handshape will change with each letter, and your palm will rotate only on certain letters. You might even stand in front of a mirror and watch as you fingerspell, to ensure you're not moving more than necessary. Keep fingerspelling the names of things in your environment.

Fingerspelling lesson 5

This lesson reviews the remaining letters: G, H, and J. The letters G and H both face inward, unlike most letters. They have the same handshape as Q and U, respectively. In G and H, the hand is rotated inward, but in Q the wrist is bent, for a downward orientation. In U, the wrist is neutral, and the fingers extend upward. The letter J is formed by first producing the letter I, then tracing the J shape in the air with your pinky finger. Note that J uses the pinky finger, but Z uses the index finger (refer back to Video Appendix A4 to review Z.). Watch Video Appendix A5 and sign along!

Here's a challenge for this lesson: You know all the letters now! For your final fingerspelling chapter, when you have some downtime, use a dictionary to look up some less common words with less frequently used letters. While you might not need these words in everyday conversation, the point—especially with your young child—is to continue developing the motor pattern needed automatically—without thinking about how to produce each letter. Fingerspell any word that comes to mind.

Appendix B: Expanded themed vocabulary

This appendix includes additional vocabulary we developed for chapters 1-4 after the initial book release. When some curriculum users requested vocabulary sheets (available on our website, ASLatHome.org), we decided to offer additional theme-based vocabulary. These words are now available to everyone!

If you're using an e-book, just click the word to see a short video (GIF) of a sign. If you're using a paperback, please scan the QR code in **Figure AB.1** to visit the Appendix B: Expanded Theme Vocabulary page.

Figure AB.1: QR code for Appendix B materials.

Chapter 1

1. POUR (e.g., to pour a drink)
2. DRINK-DOWN (i.e., to drink all of something. "You drank all of your milk!")
3. EAT-UP (i.e., to eat all of something. "You ate all of your lunch!")
4. DELICIOUS
5. GROSS (There are two versions, or regional variants, of this sign in one GIF. They have the same meaning. As you socialize more with your local deaf community, you'll get a sense of which is more common in your area.)
6. CLEAN-UP

Chapter 2

1. PLAY (This word is also now in the Chapter 6: Playtime vocabulary list.)
2. TOY (Notice this is the same as the sign PLAY above, but the handshape is the letter-T, rather than the letter-Y one.)
3. CLOTHES (This word also fits with Chapter 10: Getting Dressed.)
4. Remove hearing aids – HEARING-AID CL_XX(take off)
5. Remove cochlear implant (CI) processors – COCHLEAR-IMPLANT CL_UU(take off)
6. Remove glasses – GLASSES CL_bentL(take off)
7. Close (your) eyes – CL_L>babyO(close eyes)
8. Tilt head back – HEAD CL_S(head back)

9. Tilt head forward – <u>HEAD CL_S(head forward)</u>
10. <u>HOT</u>
11. <u>COLD</u>

Chapter 3

1. <u>POTTY</u>
2. <u>UNDERWEAR</u>
3. <u>MISTAKE</u> ("Oops/accident.")
4. Potty accident – <u>POTTY CL_O>5(liquid spread over pants)</u>
5. <u>GO TO POTTY</u>
6. <u>NEED</u>

Chapter 4

1. <u>WHO</u> (In ASL, question words such as "who," "what," "when," and "how much," are often produced at the end of a sentence and underscored by furrowed brows to indicate that you're asking a question.)
2. <u>WHERE</u>
3. <u>AGAIN</u>
4. <u>SCARY</u>
5. <u>FUNNY</u>
6. <u>HAPPY</u>
7. <u>SILLY</u>
8. <u>MAD</u>

About the Authors

Razi M. Zarchy, MS, CCC-SLP

Razi is a hearing Speech-Language Pathologist (SLP) in the Sacramento, California area, working primarily in a deaf education program. He has been an SLP since 2011. He is also a lecturer in the Communication Sciences and Disorders department at California State University, Sacramento. He is currently a doctoral student in the Doctor of Speech-Language Pathology (SLPD) program at Rocky Mountain University of Health Professions, with an anticipated graduation date of August 2023.

Leah C. Geer, PhD

Leah is a deaf Associate Professor and Program Coordinator for the ASL and Deaf Studies program at California State University, Sacramento. She has been teaching ASL since 2011 and teaches a variety of other courses at Sacramento State, including Deaf History, Deaf Culture, and Linguistics. She maintains a bilingual ASL-English "vlogBlog" and has a number of tips series on her @drz.csus Instagram page and her website, leahgeer.com.

About the Artists

Sheena Stuart-Milburn

Sheena Stuart-Milburn has called Rochester, NY, home since she obtained a bachelor's degree in Graphic Design from Rochester Institute of Technology. After graduation, Sheena embarked on a career path that saw her grow from Graphic Designer at a woman-led small business to become the Creative Director at the world's largest deaf-led non-profit, Communication Service for the Deaf (CSD). With over a decade's worth of creative design and web development under her belt, Sheena set up her own business, Design to Glow, to continue what she loves: providing top-quality visual assets and user experiences. Sheena loves to play role-playing video games, go for long walks, and spend time with her family's four cats. She is also passionate about elevating the deaf community and improving oneself through continuous learning—two big reasons why she is involved with *ASL at Home*.

Youmee Lee

Youmee Lee (she/her) is a deaf Asian American artist based in Rochester, New York. She is passionate about making information visually accessible and inviting to everybody. She is truly excited to see this book shine with her illustrations. She earned an MFA in Film and Animation from RIT in spring 2022 and looks forward to continuing her freelance career in animation and illustration post-graduation. She enjoys reading books, biking in nature, cooking international cuisines, and visiting museums and galleries.

About the Video Language Models

Romduol Ngov

Romduol Ngov is Khmer trans genderfluid deaf and a child of refugee parents. They were born in Sacramento and raised in the Bay Area. They work as a deaf interpreter. Romduol loves to go on adventures, socialize with friends and family, and spend time with their furbaby, Taylen. They are a hardcore gamer and play games in their free time after work.

Diego Guerra

Diego Guerra (pronouns they, them, theirs) is a proud native of the Rio Grande Valley in South Texas and lived in Austin, Texas for ten years. Currently, they are living in Saint Paul, Minnesota with their partner and two dogs, Rowan and Caribou. Diego works as the Community Engagement Coordinator at the National Deaf Center (NDC) and has a passion for community-based projects and programs. They are a foodie, video gamer, and sneakerhead, and they enjoy the outdoors.

Lauren Hostovsky

Lauren Hostovsky hails from Boston, Massachusetts and currently lives in Hawaii. She has worked in multiple roles such as an ASL Instructor, Early Language Specialist, and a deaf mentor to hearing families with deaf and hard of hearing children. She is passionate about her work, especially making connections with families and teaching them ASL to better support their communication with their deaf and hard of hearing children. She is excited to be on board and serve as a language model for *ASL at Home* for the second edition of the curriculum.

Tess Dozier

Tess Dozier has a bachelor's degree in social work and a master's degree in teaching ASL from the University of Northern Colorado. She has lived and worked within the deaf community of Puerto Rico in the social work, interpreting, ASL teaching, and deaf and hard of hearing teaching fields. In her free time she enjoys reading, going to the beach, and driving through scenic mountains. She is excited to serve as a language model for a trilingual curriculum that provides ASL instruction for families of deaf children that speak both English and Spanish.

References

1. U.S. Census Bureau. (n.d.). *Decennial census of population and housing.* The United States Census Bureau. Retrieved September 25, 2021, from https://www.census.gov/decennial-census

2. Dutra, N. J. (2020). *Including the deaf child at the dinner table: When and why hearing parents learn sign language* [Dissertation]. California State University, Sacramento.

3. Yosso, T. J. (2005). Whose culture has capital? A critical race theory discussion of community cultural wealth. *Race Ethnicity and Education, 8*(1), 69–91. https://doi.org/10.1080/136133205200 0341006

4. Fleischer, F., Garrow, W., & Friedman-Narr, R. (2015). Developing deaf education. In W. W. Murawski & K. L. Scott (Eds.), *What really works in secondary education.* Corwin, a SAGE company. https://sk.sagepub.com/books/what-really-works-in-secondary-education

5. Allen, T. E. (2015). ASL skills, fingerspelling ability, home communication context and early alphabetic knowledge of preschool-aged deaf children. *Sign Language Studies, 15*(3), 233–265. https://doi.org/10.1353/sls.2015.0006

6. Padden, C. A. (1996). Early bilingual lives of deaf children. In I. Parasnis (Ed.), *Cultural and language diversity and the deaf experience* (1st ed., pp. 99–116). Cambridge University Press. https://doi.org/10.1017/CBO9781139163804.007

7. Caselli, N., Pyers, J., & Lieberman, A. M. (2021). Deaf children of hearing parents have age-level vocabulary growth when exposed to American Sign Language by 6 months of age. *The Journal of Pediatrics.* https://doi.org/10.1016/j.jpeds.2021.01.029

8. Clark, J. L., & Nuccio, J. (2020). Protactile linguistics: Discussing recent research findings. *Journal of American Sign Languages and Literatures.* https://journalofasl.com/protactile-linguistics/

9. Edwards, T. (2014). From compensation to integration: Effects of the pro-tactile movement on the sublexical structure of Tactile American Sign Language. *Journal of Pragmatics, 69*, 22–41. https://doi.org/10.1016/j.pragma.2014.05.005

10. Edwards, T., & Brentari, D. (2020). Feeling phonology: The conventionalization of phonology in Protactile communities in the United States. *Language, 96*(4), 819–840.

11. Edwards, T., & Brentari, D. (2021). The grammatical incorporation of demonstratives in an emerging tactile language. *Frontiers in Psychology, 11*, 3258. https://doi.org/10.3389/fpsyg.2020.579992

12. Petronio, K., & Dively, V. (2006). YES, #NO, visibility, and variation in ASL and Tactile ASL. *Sign Language Studies, 7*(1), 57–98.

13. Mitchell, R. E., & Karchmer, M. (2004). Chasing the mythical ten percent: Parental hearing status of deaf and hard of hearing students in the United States. *Sign Language Studies, 4*(2), 138–163.

14. Braun, D. C., Gormally, C., & Clark, M. D. (2017). The deaf mentoring survey: A community cultural wealth framework for measuring mentoring effectiveness with underrepresented students. *CBE–*

Life Sciences Education, 16(1), ar10. https://doi.org/10.1187/cbe.15-07-0155

15. Johnson, S., Stapleton, L., & Berrett, B. (2020). Deaf Community Cultural Wealth in community college students. *The Journal of Deaf Studies and Deaf Education, 25*(4), 438–446. https://doi.org/10.1093/deafed/enaa016

16. De Meulder, M. (2018). "So, why do you sign?" Deaf and hearing new signers, their motivation, and revitalisation policies for sign languages. *Applied Linguistics Review, 10*(4), 705–724. https://doi.org/10.1515/applirev-2017-0100

17. Pizer, G., Walters, K., & Meier, R. P. (2007). Bringing up baby with baby signs: Language ideologies and socialization in hearing families. *Sign Language Studies, 7*(4), 387–430. https://doi.org/10.1353/sls.2007.0026

18. Robinson, O., & Henner, J. (2018). Authentic voices, authentic encounters: Cripping the university through American Sign Language. *Disability Studies Quarterly, 38*(4), Article 4. http://dx.doi.org/10.18061/dsq.v38i4.6111

19. Snoddon, K. (2014). Baby sign as deaf gain. In H.-D. L. Bauman & J. Murray (Eds.), *Deaf gain: Raising the stakes for human diversity.* University of Minnesota Press. http://www.jstor.org/stable/10.5749/j.ctt9qh3m7

20. Humphries, T., Kushalnagar, P., Mathur, G., Napoli, D. J., Padden, C., Rathmann, C., & Smith, S. R. (2012). Language acquisition for deaf children: Reducing the harms of zero tolerance to the use of alternative approaches. *Harm Reduction Journal, 9*, 16. https://doi.org/10.1186/1477-7517-9-16

21. Center for Early Literacy Learning. (2010). *Talk to me…in parentese!* Infant Practice Guides for Parents. http://www.earlyliteracylearning.org/cellpract_parent/infants/PG_1_I_Talk2Me.pdf

22. Pizer, G., Meier, R. P., & Points, K. S. (2011). Child-directed signing as a linguistic register. In R. Channon & H. van der Hulst (Eds.), *Formational Units in Sign Languages* (pp. 65–86). de Gruyter. https://doi.org/10.1515/9781614510680.65

23. Masataka, N. (1996). Perception of motherese in a signed language by 6-month-old deaf infants. *Developmental Psychology, 32*(5), 874–879. https://psycnet.apa.org/record/1996-01792-008

24. Masataka, N. (1998). Perception of motherese in Japanese Sign Language by 6-month-old hearing infants. *Developmental Psychology, 34*(2), 241–246. https://doi.org/10.1037//0012-1649.34.2.241

25. Reilly, J. S., & Bellugi, U. (1996). Competition on the face: Affect and language in ASL motherese. *Journal of Child Language, 23*(1), 219–239. https://doi.org/10.1017/S0305000900010163

26. Sanford Koester, L., & Lahti-Harper, E. (2010). Mother-infant hearing status and intuitive parenting behaviors during the first 18 months. *American Annals of the Deaf, 155*(1), 5–18. https://doi.org/10.1353/aad.0.0134

27. Shelden, M. L., & Rush, D. D. (2001). The ten myths about providing early intervention services in natural environments. *Inf Young Children, 14*(1), 1–13.

28. Hwang, A.-W., Chao, M.-Y., & Liu, S.-W. (2013). A randomized controlled trial of routines-based early intervention for children with or at risk for developmental delay. *Research in Developmental*

Disabilities, 34(10), 3112–3123. https://doi.org/10.1016/j.ridd.2013.06.037

29. McWilliam, R. A. (2016). The routines-based model for supporting speech and language. *Revista de Logopedia, Foniatría y Audiología, 36*(4), 178–184. https://doi.org/10.1016/j.rlfa.2016.07.005

30. Yorkston, K., Dowden, P., Honsinger, M., Marriner, N., & Smith, K. (1988). A comparison of standard and user vocabulary lists. *Augmentative and Alternative Communication, 4*(4), 189–210. https://doi.org/10.1080/07434618812331274807

31. Banajee, M., Dicarlo, C., & Buras Stricklin, S. (2003). Core vocabulary determination for toddlers. *Augmentative and Alternative Communication, 19*(2), 67–73. https://doi.org/10.1080/0743461031000112034

32. Boenisch, J., & Soto, G. (2015). The oral core vocabulary of typically developing English-speaking school-aged children: Implications for AAC practice. *Augmentative and Alternative Communication, 31*(1), 77–84. https://doi.org/10.3109/07434618.2014.1001521

33. Tennant, R. A., & Brown, M. G. (2010). *The American Sign Language handshape dictionary.* Gallaudet University Press. http://gupress.gallaudet.edu/bookpage/ASLD2bookpage.html

34. The Editors of Gallaudet University Press, & Gordon, J. M. (2014). *The Gallaudet children's dictionary of American Sign Language.* Gallaudet University Press. https://gcdasl.com/

35. Pudans-Smith, K. K., Cue, K. R., Wolsey, J.-L. A., & Clark, M. D. (2019). *To Deaf or not to deaf: That is the question. Psychology, 10*(15), 2091–2114. https://doi.org/10.4236/psych.2019.1015135

36. Hochgesang, J., Crasborn, O., & Lillo-Martin, D. (2021). *ASL Signbank.* New Haven, CT: Haskins Lab, Yale University. https://aslsignbank.haskins.yale.edu/

37. DesJardin, J. L., & Eisenberg, L. S. (2007). Maternal contributions: Supporting language development in young children with cochlear implants. *Ear and Hearing, 28*(4), 456–469. https://doi.org/10.1097/AUD.0b013e31806dc1ab

38. Rajesh, V., & Venkatesh, L. (2019). Preliminary evaluation of a low-intensity parent training program on speech-language stimulation for children with language delay. *International Journal of Pediatric Otorhinolaryngology, 122*, 99–104. https://doi.org/10.1016/j.ijporl.2019.03.034

39. Lund, E. (2018). The effects of parent training on vocabulary scores of young children with hearing loss. *American Journal of Speech-Language Pathology, 27*(2), 765–777. https://doi.org/10.1044/2018_AJSLP-16-0239

40. Kolb, R. (2016). The deaf body in public space. *New York Times.* https://www.nytimes.com/2016/09/28/opinion/the-deaf-body-in-public-space.html

41. Kantor, R. (1980). The acquisition of classifiers in American Sign Language. *Sign Language Studies, 28*(1), 193–208. https://muse.jhu.edu/issue/27477

42. Zwisterlood, I. (2012). Classifiers. In R. Pfau, M. Steinbach, & B. Woll (Eds.), *Sign language: An international handbook* (Vol. 37). De Gruyter Mouton. https://doi.org/10.1515/9783110261325

43. Girolametto, L., Weitzman, E., Wiigs, M., & Pearce, P. S. (1999). The relationship between maternal

language measures and language development in toddlers with expressive vocabulary delays. *American Journal of Speech-Language Pathology, 8*(4), 364–374. https://doi.org/10.1044/1058-0360.0804.364

44. Girolametto, L., Pearce, P. S., & Weitzman, E. (2016). The effects of focused stimulation for promoting vocabulary in young children with delays: A pilot study. *Journal of Children's Communication Development.* https://doi.org/10.1177/152574019501700205

45. Huttenlocher, J., Haight, W., Bryk, A., Seltzer, M., & Lyons, T. (1991). Early vocabulary growth: Relation to language input and gender. *Developmental Psychology, 27*(2), 236–248. https://doi.org/10.1037/0012-1649.27.2.236

46. Petitto, L. A., Berens, M. S., Kovelman, I., Dubins, M. H., Jasinska, K., & Shalinsky, M. (2012). The "Perceptual Wedge Hypothesis" as the basis for bilingual babies' phonetic processing advantage: New insights from fNIRS brain imaging. *Brain and Language, 121*(2), 130–143. https://doi.org/10.1016/j.bandl.2011.05.003

47. Davidson, K., Lillo-Martin, D., & Chen Pichler, D. (2013). Spoken English language development among native signing children with cochlear implants. *Journal of Deaf Studies and Deaf Education, 19*(2), 238–250. https://doi.org/10.1093/deafed/ent045

48. Hall, W. C. (2017). What you don't know can hurt you: The risk of language deprivation by impairing sign language development in deaf children. *Maternal and Child Health Journal, 21*(5), 961–965. https://doi.org/10.1007/s10995-017-2287-y

49. Roberts, M. Y., & Hampton, L. H. (2018). Exploring cascading effects of multimodal communication skills in infants with hearing loss. *The Journal of Deaf Studies and Deaf Education, 23*(1), 95–105. https://doi.org/10.1093/deafed/enx041

50. DesJardin, J. L., Doll, E. R., Stika, C. J., Eisenberg, L. S., Johnson, K. J., Ganguly, D. H., Colson, B. G., & Henning, S. C. (2014). Parental support for language development during joint book reading for young children with hearing loss. *Communication Disorders Quarterly, 35*(3), 167–181. https://doi.org/10.1177/1525740113518062

51. Kaiser, A. P., & Hancock, T. B. (2003). Teaching parents new skills to support their young children's development. *Infants & Young Children, 16*(1), 9–21. https://journals.lww.com/iycjournal/fulltext/2003/01000/teaching_parents_new_skills_to_support_their_young.3.aspx

52. Curtin, M., Dirks, E., Cruice, M., Herman, R., Newman, L., Rodgers, L., & Morgan, G. (2021). Assessing parent behaviours in parent–child interactions with deaf and hard of hearing infants aged 0–3 years: A systematic review. *Journal of Clinical Medicine, 10*(15), 3345. https://doi.org/10.3390/jcm10153345

53. McDuffie, A., & Yoder, P. (2010). Types of parent verbal responsiveness that predict language in young children with autism spectrum disorder. *Journal of Speech, Language, and Hearing Research, 53*(4), 1026–1039. https://doi.org/10.1044/1092-4388(2009/09-0023)

54. Tomasello, M., & Farrar, M. J. (1986). Joint attention and early language. *Child Development, 57*(6), 1454–1463. https://doi.org/10.2307/1130423

55. Brooks, R., Singleton, J. L., & Meltzoff, A. N. (2020). Enhanced gaze-following behavior in Deaf infants of Deaf parents. *Developmental Science, 23*(2). https://doi.org/10.1111/desc.12900

56. Holzrichter, A. S., & Meier, R. P. (1999). Child-directed signing in American Sign Language. In C. Chamberlain, J. P. Morford, & R. I. Mayberry (Eds.), *Language acquisition by eye*. Psychology Press.

57. Bosworth, R. G., & Stone, A. (2021). Rapid development of perceptual gaze control in hearing native signing infants and children. *Developmental Science, 24*(4), e13086. https://doi.org/10.1111/desc.13086

58. Battison, R. M. (2003). *Lexical borrowing in American Sign Language*. Linstock Press.

59. Keane, J., Brentari, D., & Riggle, J. (2012). Coarticulation in ASL fingerspelling. *Proceedings of the North East Linguistic Society, 42*. http://pubs.jonkeane.com/pdfs/Keane2012aa.pdf

60. Morford, J. P., & MacFarlane, J. (2003). Frequency characteristics of American Sign Language. *Sign Language Studies, 3*(2), 213–225. https://doi.org/10.1353/sls.2003.0003

61. Roberts, M. Y., Kaiser, A. P., Wolfe, C. E., Bryant, J. D., & Spidalieri, A. M. (2014). Effects of the Teach-Model-Coach-Review instructional approach on caregiver use of language support strategies and children's expressive language skills. *Journal of Speech, Language, and Hearing Research, 57*(5), 1851–1869. https://doi.org/10.1044/2014_JSLHR-L-13-0113

62. Sigafoos, J., Drasgow, E., Reichle, J., O'Reilly, M., Green, V. A., & Tait, K. (2004). Tutorial: Teaching communicative rejecting to children with severe disabilities. *American Journal of Speech-Language Pathology, 13*(1), 31–42. https://doi.org/10.1044/1058-0360(2004/005)

63. Zelinsky, N. A. M., & Shadish, W. (2018). A demonstration of how to do a meta-analysis that combines single-case designs with between-groups experiments: The effects of choice making on challenging behaviors performed by people with disabilities. *Developmental Neurorehabilitation, 21*(4), 266–278. https://doi.org/10.3109/17518423.2015.1100690

64. Benedict, R., & Stecker, E. (2011). Early intervention: The missing link. *Journal of American Sign Languages and Literatures*. https://journalofasl.com/ei/

65. Mayberry, R. I. (2007). When timing is everything: Age of first-language acquisition effects on second-language learning. *Applied Psycholinguistics, 28*(3), 537–549. https://doi.org/10.1017/S0142716407070294

66. Sussman, F. (n.d.). *The power of using everyday routines to promote young children's language and social skills*. The Hanen Centre. Retrieved July 27, 2021, from http://www.hanen.org/helpful-info/articles/power-of-using-everyday-routines.aspx

67. Weitzman, E. (2017). *It takes two to talk: A practical guide for parents of children with language delays (Fifth edition)*. Hanen Centre. http://www.hanen.org/Guidebooks/Parents/It-Takes-Two-to-Talk.aspx

68. Wilson, M., & Wilson, T. P. (2005). An oscillator model of the timing of turn-taking. *Psychonomic Bulletin & Review, 12*(6), 957–968. https://doi.org/10.3758/BF03206432

69. Nguyen, T., Schleihauf, H., Kayhan, E., Matthes, D., Vrtička, P., & Hoehl, S. (2021). Neural synchrony in mother-child conversation: Exploring the role of conversation patterns. *Social Cognitive and Affective Neuroscience, 16*(1–2), 93–102. https://doi.org/10.1093/scan/nsaa079

70. Stanton-Chapman, T. L., & Snell, M. E. (2011). Promoting turn-taking skills in preschool children with disabilities: The effects of a peer-based social communication intervention. *Early Childhood Research Quarterly, 26*(3), 303–319. https://doi.org/10.1016/j.ecresq.2010.11.002

71. Horrell, R. M. (2021, October 3). *When I was teaching 6th grade at a mainstream school.* Facebook Comment. https://www.facebook.com/razi.zarchy/posts/421045249440185

72. Hameed, K., & Howard, J. (2021). A *clinical perspective on talking to kids about racism: How to speak openly and tackle hard questions.* Child Mind Institute. https://childmind.org/article/a-clinical-perspective-on-talking-to-kids-about-racism/

73. Individuals with Disabilities Education Act, 20 U.S.C. § 1400 *et seq.* (2004). https://sites.ed.gov/idea/statute-chapter-33/

74. Cleave, P. L., Becker, S. D., Curran, M. K., Van Horne, A. J. O., & Fey, M. E. (2015). The efficacy of recasts in language intervention: A systematic review and meta-analysis. *American Journal of Speech-Language Pathology, 24*(2), 237–255. https://doi.org/10.1044/2015_AJSLP-14-0105

75. Sultana, N., Wong, L. L. N., & Purdy, S. C. (2019). Analysis of amount and style of oral interaction related to language outcomes in children with hearing loss: A systematic review (2006–2016). *Journal of Speech, Language, and Hearing Research, 62*(9), 3470–3492. https://doi.org/10.1044/2019_JSLHR-L-19-0076

76. *What is De'VIA.* (2015, July 14). De'VIA Curriculum. https://deviacurr.wordpress.com/devia-curr/what-is-devia/

77. Akamatsu, C. T. (1985). Fingerspelling formulae: A word is more or less than the sum of its letters. In W. Stokoe & V. Volterra (Eds.), *Sign Language Research* (pp. 126–132). Linstock Press.

78. Padden, C. A. (2005). Learning to fingerspell twice: Young signing children's acquisition of fingerspelling. In B. Schick, M. Marschark, & P. E. Spencer (Eds.), *Advances in the Sign-Language Development of Deaf Children.* Oxford University Press. https://doi.org/10.1093/acprof:oso/9780195180947.003.0008

79. Haptonstall-Nykaza, T. S., & Schick, B. (2007). The transition from fingerspelling to English print: Facilitating English decoding. *Journal of Deaf Studies and Deaf Education, 12*(2), 172–183. https://doi.org/10.1093/deafed/enm003

80. Scott, J. A., Hansen, S. G., & Lederberg, A. R. (2019). Fingerspelling and print: Understanding the word reading of deaf children. *American Annals of the Deaf, 164*(4), 429–449. https://doi.org/10.1353/aad.2019.0026

Made in the USA
Las Vegas, NV
13 December 2023

82774778R00070